HOW TO WRITE SIGNS, TICKETS AND POSTERS

WITH NUMEROUS ENGRAVINGS AND DIAGRAMS

Edited By

PAUL N. HASLUCK

First published in 1899

PAUL NOONCREE HASLUCK

Paul Nooncree Hasluck was born in April 1854, in South Australia. The third son of Lewis Hasluck, of Perth, the family moved to the UK when Hasluck was still young. He subsequently lived in Herne Bay (Kent), before moving to 120 Victoria Street, London, later in life.

Hasluck was the secretary of the 'Institution of Sanitary Engineers' – an organisation dedicated to promoting knowledge of, and development in the field of urban sanitation. Hasluck was also the editor of several magazines and volumes over his lifetime, including *Work Handbooks,* and *Building World.* He was an eminently knowledgeable and talented engineer, and wrote many practical books. These included such titles as; *Lathe-Work: A Practical Treatise on the Tools employed in the Art of Turning* (1881), *The Watch-Jobber's Handy Book* (1887), *Screw-Threads, and Methods of Producing Them* (1887), and an eight volume series on *The Automobile* as well as a staggering eighteen volumes of *Mechanics Manuals.*

In his personal life, Hasluck married in 1883, to 'Florence' and the two enjoyed a happy marriage, though his wife unfortunately died young, in 1916. Hasluck himself died on 7th May, 1931, aged seventy-seven.

CONTENTS

LIST OF ILLUSTRATIONS

SIGNS, TICKETS, AND POSTERS

CHAPTER I.

INTRODUCTORY AND PRELIMINARY PRACTICE.

THE use of signs as a means of advertising is of very ancient origin. In old Rome the taverns had signs, and the Greeks also made use of them, as is proved by allusions made by the old Greek writers on the subject. In England, during the middle ages, when most people could neither read nor write, a sign, or signboard, was of absolute necessity to the tradesman. These were generally indicative of the trade carried on within. With the spread of education these signs gradually fell into disuse ; still many exist to the present day, as the three golden balls of the pawnbroker and the gaily-painted pole of the barber. The modern practice of sign-painting—accepting the term in its original sense—is an almost obsolete art, which survives only in the royal arms, arms of public companies, heraldic shields, and in some hotel sign-boards. It is, however, the modern practice of lettering on signs, shop-fronts, walls, vehicles, etc., that will be dealt with in this handbook. The precise name of this art has invariably presented a difficulty with previous writers on the subject, but the present title sufficiently describes the work, as now practised. There are three distinct classes of work, sign-painting, sign-writing, and lettering.

The sign-painter is an artist capable, as a rule, of doing any class of letter painting. The sign-writer is capable of doing any class of writing and lettering, from church work to the outside of a tradesman's shop, but stopping short of pictorial work. The letterer may be an ordinary painter, who is able to exactly form letters and numerals, and who by practice acquires consider-able skill. Men of this last class are to be found working in wheelwrights' and carriage-builders' yards, and in the railway-carriage and waggon works through-out the country. They generally use block letters, simply shaded, such as one sees on railway waggons and coal trucks. This work is simply letter painting. It has much sameness about it, and holds out small field for improvement in the way of spacing, style and display. Probably many of these letter painters, after a little training, would be able to execute sign-writing with credit.

It must not be inferred from what has been said that it requires a gifted nature to properly acquire the art of sign-writing, for with proper and methodical training it is within the reach of all. Indeed, it will be shown how the more simple styles of plain lettering may be carried out by almost mechanical means. The instructions, however, are principally intended for those who follow some trade in which a little lettering is sometimes required, and thus the workman has a chance to learn, by properly following up the course of instruction laid down in these pages.

It is very essential that the sign-writer should acquire some practical knowledge of freehand drawing and geometry. A little only is better than none at all ; but the more the student knows the more will he be a master of his art. It is not necessary to draw copies exactly the same size as they are given in these pages, although, for the purpose of training his eye, he should for some time endeavour to draw them to the same scale, and then ascertain by measurement how far his completed drawing is out. Afterwards it is neces-sary to become proficient in both reducing and enlarging, and after awhile the student should make each drawing larger than the preceding one, and taking this last as copy for the next one. He can thus go on until the limits of a full-sized sheet of drawing paper are reached, so that when the time comes to practise upon the black-board he will gradually have worked up to the enlargements almost without being aware of it. All these intermediate drawings should be kept as copies to practise from on his blackboard, and it will be a good plan to practise until he actually makes a drawing on the blackboard enlarged direct from the illustrations in these pages, and when doing this he should put his intermediate drawings out of sight.

To commence a short series of drawing lessons, the

Fig. 1.—Perpendicular Straight Lines.

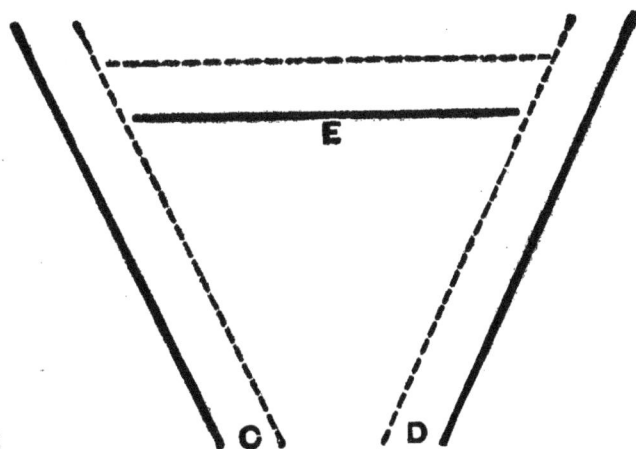

Fig. 2.—Horizontal and Oblique Straight Lines.

student should provide himself with a few sheets of common drawing paper, a twopenny HB pencil, and a piece of indiarubber. The paper should be pinned to a drawing board. The sign-writer must learn to draw in a bold, fearless style, straight, horizontal, perpendicular and oblique lines, and afterwards graceful curves. These are the first exercises in freehand drawing, and until they are thoroughly mastered it is useless to attempt to proceed further.

To do good work, the pencil—that being the first tool the draughtsman will handle—must be properly pointed, as shown on p. 136. Then let him draw a perpendicular straight line, A, in Fig. 1, which may be done the more easily by first marking it out as a dotted line, B,

and afterwards filling it in with a firm, decided stroke
from top to bottom. Horizontal and oblique lines are

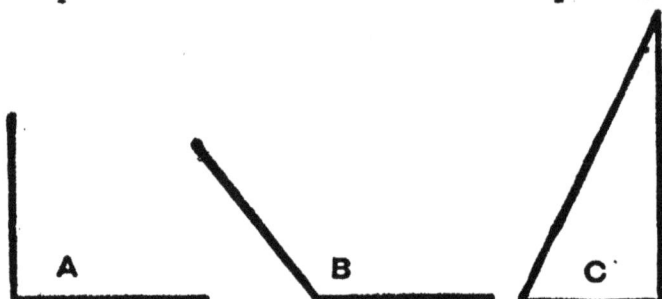

Fig. 3.—Various Angles.

Fig. 4.—Parallel Lines.

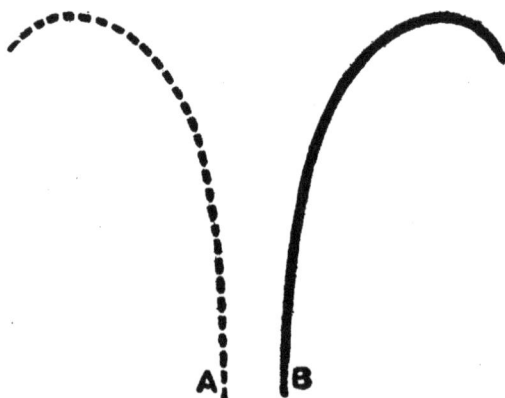

Fig. 5.—Simple Curves.

to be practised in the same way as shown in the
examples c, d, e, in Fig. 2. Lines should also be drawn
to meet each other at right, acute, and obtuse angles, as
illustrated at A. B. C, in Fig. 3. Drawing parallel lines

Fig. 4) should also be practised. The student must next pay attention to simple curved lines, A, B (Fig. 5), and to

Fig. 6.—Compound Curves.

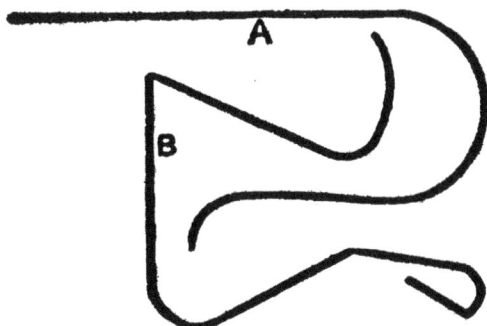

Fig. 7.—Simple Curved and Straight Lines.

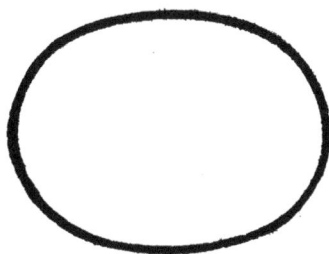

Fig. 8.—Circle.   Fig. 9.—Oval.

compound curves, C, D, E (Fig. 6). Practice is continued with straight and curved compound lines (Fig. 7), which may either be continuous or broken ; and, following these, the circle and oval (Figs. 8 and 9) must be taken in hand.

This initial stage is the most uninteresting part of our work, and it needs great patience, but if persevered in, the learner will be amply rewarded in the near future. In order to give variety to the drawing lessons, the learner may presently proceed to copy, until perfect, such subjects as are shown in Figs. 10, 11, and 12, all of

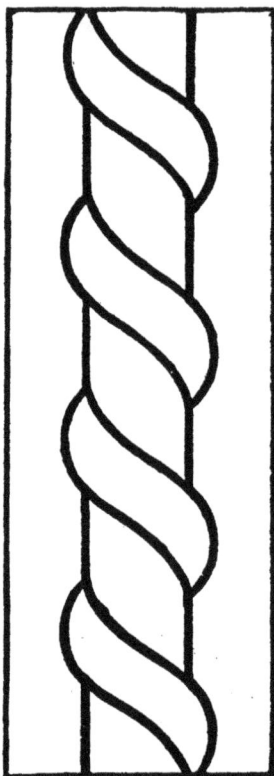

Fig. 10.—Freehand Drawn Coil Round Cylinder.

Fig. 11—Freehand Drawn Cable Twist.

which immediately concern the subject of this handbook. They are given merely as copies for incessant practice, and need no description.   These should be followed with the alphabet drawn within faint-lined squares.

It will be helpful here to learn descriptive definitions of those geometrical terms with which the sign-writer should be quite familiar.

Geometrical problems would be out of place here, but

the learner of the art of sign-writing should obtain a
good treatise on plane geometry, and carefully work out
those problems which are likely to prove serviceable to

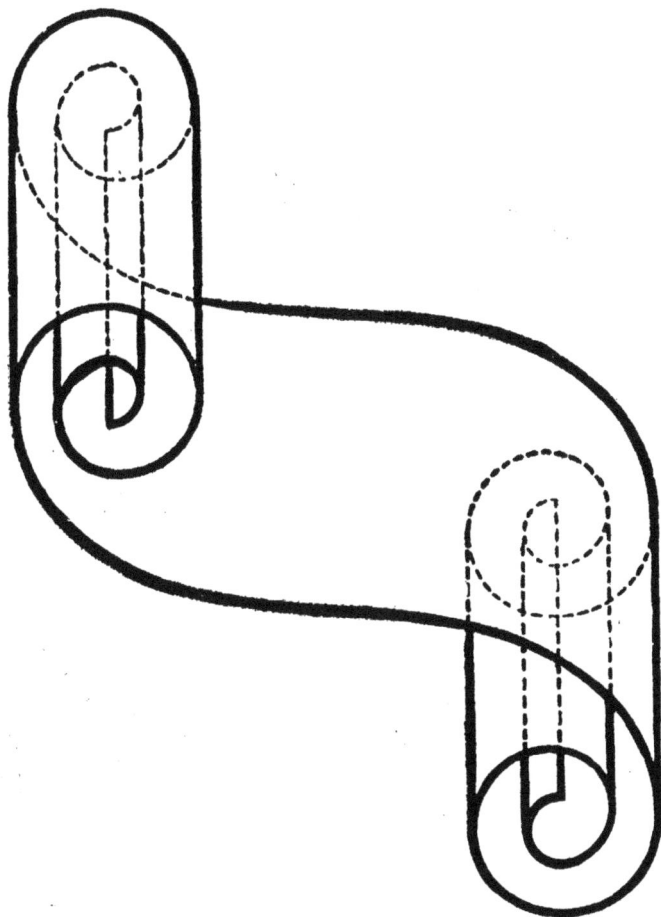

Fig. 12.—Freehand Drawn Scroll for Inscription.

him in his work. Elementary problems are those which
he will find most useful.

As we shall have occasion to use a blackboard for
future lessons, the following directions for making one,
similar to the board shown in Fig. 13, will be useful.
Procure a good, thoroughly dry and well-seasoned yellow
deal board, measuring 10 ft. long, 9 in. wide and ⅞ in.
thick. Also another board of the same wood, 12 ft. by

9 in. by 1 in., to provide the legs and cross pieces of the
stand, as shown in the illustration.

Take the ⅞ in. board and square both ends ; saw those

Fig. 13.—Sign-Writer's Blackboard and Easel.

off, leaving the board just 9 ft. long, and then saw
this into three equal lengths ; these should then be
tongued and grooved in a workmanlike manner, glued and
clamped up until dry.

The frame consists of the two legs, the centre-piece

and the two cross pieces. These should be put together with mortise and tenon joints, and finally well screwed on to the back of the boards, and the hind leg attached with an ordinary "butt" hinge. The board must now have several coats of paint, containing plenty of driers, and must be well sand-papered and allowed to rest between each coat. When thoroughly dry it is fit for use, and should be in constant demand for free-hand sketching, lettering, and working out original designs.

An arrangement that will possibly be found to be more convenient is to let the frame form an easel, the board being supported on pegs inserted in holes in the framework, as shown in Fig. 13.

Lettering is merely a special class of drawing, more or less advanced, according to the proficiency attained in the higher orders of ornamental lettering; thus a good deal of practice, after the plan laid down in the preceding pages, is absolutely necessary.

One of the best examples for practice in freehand drawing the pupil in lettering could have placed before him is the drawing of circles. Of course, a perfectly true circle is quickest drawn with the aid of compasses, and these are always used in actual work, though it is possible to produce one with the hand, guided by the eye alone. This entails close application and constant practice, but success in course of time is an ensured certainty. Perhaps one of the best methods of educating the hand and the eye, and of enabling the former to obey the dictates of the latter, is repeated practice in drawing the circle in all sizes, and without any extra-neous aid.

Almost every sign-writer has his own individual method of procedure ; but whatever this may be, he must, before he proceeds to "chalk in" his work, picture to himself, to a certain degree, the size, shape and construction of the letters, and the hand obeys the eye accordingly. The proper and methodical training of the hand and eye will, it is hoped, be followed by the student with due appreciation, as it is an important matter often entirely overlooked.

The illustrated examples of freehand drawing and outline subjects on pp. 11–15 have been selected for the special purpose we have in view, but as the novice has been so urgently advised to diligently practise drawing the circle, some remarks should be made on the best method of proceeding to this work.

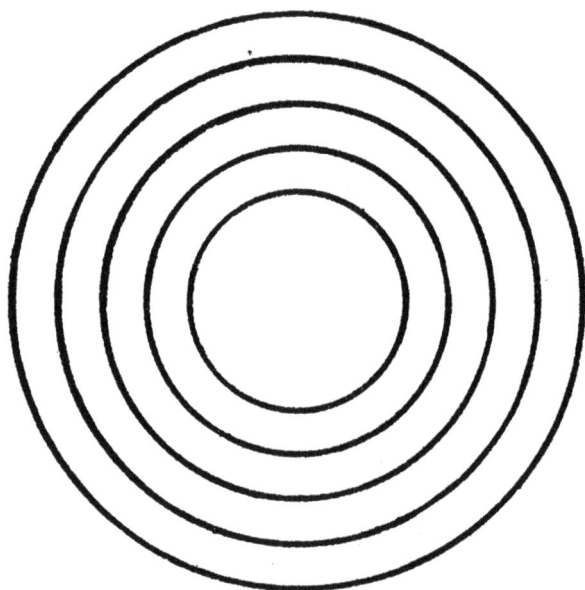

Fig 14.—Concentric Circles.

It is easier to draw a small circle than a large one. The beginner should therefore start by describing a circle about three inches in diameter, persevering until he is able to draw it, time after time, with tolerable correctness. This is best done with slate pencil, on a large slate, which should not be allowed to lie upon the table, but should be nearly upright, propped up with books, held by the left hand, or, better still, placed on a small easel, which is easily constructed.

Having made satisfactory progress with small circles, draw a circle three inches in diameter and then larger ones outside this, and all at a given distance apart, as shown in Fig. 14, until the whole surface of the slate is covered. Larger circles may afterwards be drawn upon the blackboard with both chalk and brush, but the student must not confine himself to any one class of work, but should change from one subject to another, for the sake of variety and interest.

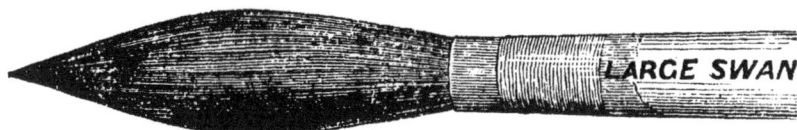

Fig. 15.

Fig. 16.

Fig. 17.

Fig. 18.

Fig. 19.

Fig. 20.

Figs. 15 to 20.—Camel-Hair Writers.

Having tired of pencil and paper, the student next brings his blackboard into requisition. He will also require a few white demonstration chalks—these are tapered chalks four inches long, and are more expensive than the ordinary blackboard chalk, which would be of no use for our purpose ; a camel-hair writer (Figs. 15 to 20), a thin piece of planed board to act as a palette, and some zinc white paint thinned to the proper consistency with a little sweet oil, and some old dusters or rags. Palettes of various forms are illustrated by Figs. 21 to 24.

After the pupil has practised for some hours on the blackboard with chalk, and has redrawn each subject several times over, he should practise with his camel-

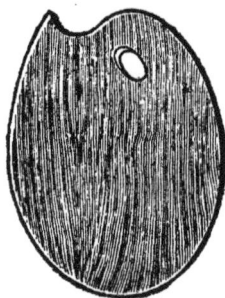

Fig. 21.

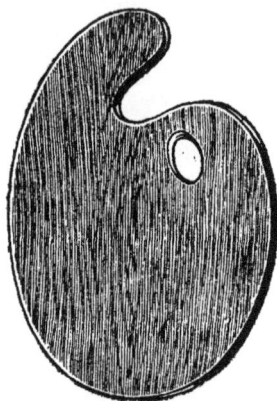

Fig. 22.

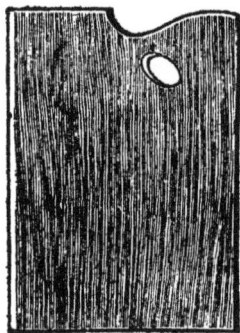

Fig. 23.

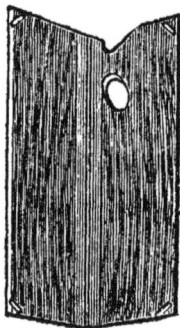

Fig. 24.

Figs. 21 to 24.—Palettes.

hair writer. Having worked a little white paint on to his extemporised palette, and thoroughly cleaned the chalk marks from the black board, all the freehand subjects should be drawn with the brush and paint, commencing with straight lines and curves. His first effort is to make with his camel-hair writer a line of the same thickness throughout. He may use a mahl stick to rest the wrist upon, or may rest his right hand on the left wrist, the left hand being placed against the board. If his hand is sufficiently steady and firm he had better dispense with all these aids in his preliminary work; afterwards he will be the better able to appreciate the help of a mahl stick, though this is never absolutely necessary for a man with a steady hand.

The lines should be made, as far as possible, with the point of the brush, and not with the side. Work with a bold, unhesitating hand, to give a firm and finished appearance to the work. Any timidity or hesitancy will

Fig. 25.—Pair of Tin Dippers.

at once betray the hand of the novice. The white paint should be of just such a consistency as to flow freely and evenly from the brush, and at the same time give sufficient covering power on the board. The brush is held in much the same way as a pen in ordinary writing; it should not be grasped tightly, as the strain on the sinews of the hand tends to cramp it, and this very soon tires the hand and so renders it unsteady. When the board has been covered with paint marks, it must immediately be wiped clean with a piece of rag, which has previously been steeped in a little common turpentine. It is as well to have the paint in a tin dipper, such as shown at Fig. 25 and on p. 40.

The student should not confine himself to the examples given here, but should draw anything that comes in his way that is likely to be of use to him. He will find plenty of other subjects in books and illustrated advertisements, and even on the poster hoardings in the street. He should also go round, book in hand, and make sketches of any little bits of good work over shop fronts and other places of business to which he may take a fancy, afterwards making finished drawings of them at home for future use and practice. Practising in this way will prove of great assistance to the student in his course of self-tuition.

CHAPTER II.

THE FORMATION OF LETTERS, STOPS, AND NUMERALS.

A GREAT aid to successful sign-writing is a study of the principles upon which the letters, numerals, and stops of a block alphabet are constructed. Before going in detail over the formation of these, it may be as well to point out that it is not intended that in the actual writing of a ticket the mechanical measurements, etc., given should be followed; yet, at the outset, it will be well if a complete alphabet, with the stops and numerals, be drawn, character by character, on separate pieces of paper by the method now to be indicated. By the time this course has been gone through, the learner will have acquired quite a readiness in the formation of letters which would be vainly sought in desultory copying and sketching of this, that, and another example that may turn up haphazard.

It might be thought by a casual observer that the several letters of an alphabet have little in common except that they come between the same pair of parallel lines—that is, they are all of the same height. Besides this, they bear throughout their structure definite relative proportions, which must be observed in order to produce artistic writing. With the exception of **I**, **W**, and **M**, all the letters of one alphabet may be drawn in the same-sized rectangle, the sides of which touch the limits of the letters. Figs. 26 to 29, are monograms forming an alphabet, and showing the interdependence of the limbs on each letter.

Block letters are those most generally in use. They are the most effective for business tickets, labels for museum and cabinet specimens, and all work where legibility rather than ornament is wanted.

In the examples here given, the limb-width of the letters is one-sixth of their height. This makes a very good proportion for all bold, business-like writing. When the limb-width is excessively thin as compared with the height, letters have a spindly and undecided look, and do not attract the eye so well. When very thick, they have a clumsy, unformed appearance, which makes them difficult to read. The letter-width here used is nine-twelfths of the letter-height.

Take each letter in order of its simplicity, commencing with I. About this there is no difficulty; it is merely a rectangular character, the height and width of which determine the height and limb-width of the others. L, F, E, H, and T contain the element I, combined with one, two, or three horizontal limbs. L is a left-hand upright, joined to a horizontal limb at the bottom, going right across. F has the same limb as L, but it forms a cross-bar at the top instead of the bottom, and a cross-bar midway between top and bottom, reaching five-eighths across from left to right. E is merely F with L's cross-limb added. H is a right I, a left I, and a cross-bar joining them halfway between top and bottom. T is an I midway between right and left, with the top cross-bar of E added. T frequently has its cross-limb made to exceed the general width of cross-bars, to satisfy the eye, and counteract the tendency T has to appear not wide enough. H is likewise often made a little narrower, to counteract its tendency to appear too wide. These and several other deviations from hard-and-fast rule will be taken up by the learner as progress is made; they can be disregarded for the present. V has two slanting limbs; and here let it be noted that the width of slanting limbs is measured at right angles to their length, as 1, 2 (Fig. 26), not at their junction with the enclosing rectangle, as 3, 4. To form V, find 5, the central point at the bottom, and from 5, on each side, mark 6 and 7, both being distant from 5 to the extent of three-fourths of the limb-width. From 6 draw the line, 6, 8 ; and from 7 draw the line, 7, 4.

Measure 1, 2, the limb-width, at right angles to 7, 4, and draw 3, 10 and 9, 10 to meet at 10. A is an inverted V with a cross-bar added to it. The cross-bar is drawn so that its *centre* line, shown by the dashes 11, 12, is one-third up from the bottom. Many amateur writers err in making this cross-bar half-way up. X is made by finding 15, the centre of the rectangle

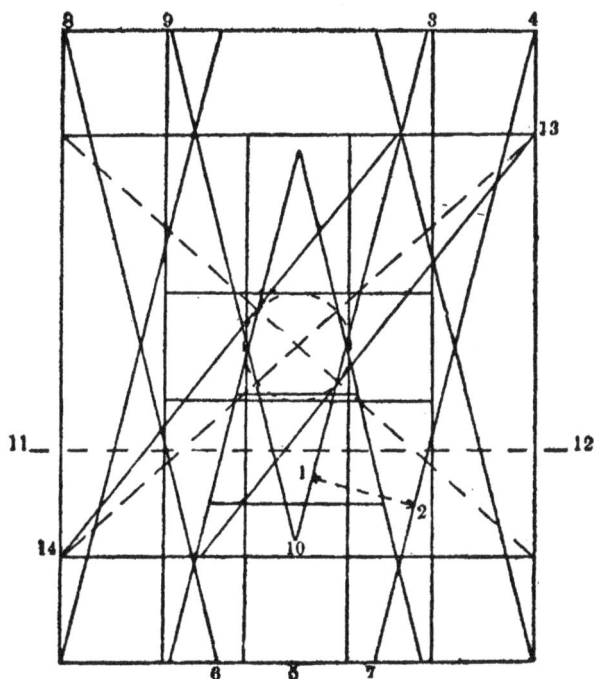

Fig. 26.—Monogram showing how to draw the letters
I, L, F, E, H, T, A, V, and Z.

(Fig. 27). This centre is the point where lines 16, 17 18, and 19 cross.

Round the centre, 15, draw the circle shown, with diameter equal to limb-width. This will require the compass points to be half limb-width apart. Place the straight-edge to pass through 16, a corner of the rect-angle, and place the pencil point in position there, ready to draw a line. Keeping its edge against the

pencil, turn the straight-edge about, until it also touches
the circle ; then draw the line 16, 20.   Treat the three
other corners in the same way, drawing lines from them
to touch the circle, and to pass on to the limits of the
rectangle at points 20, 21, 22, and 23.

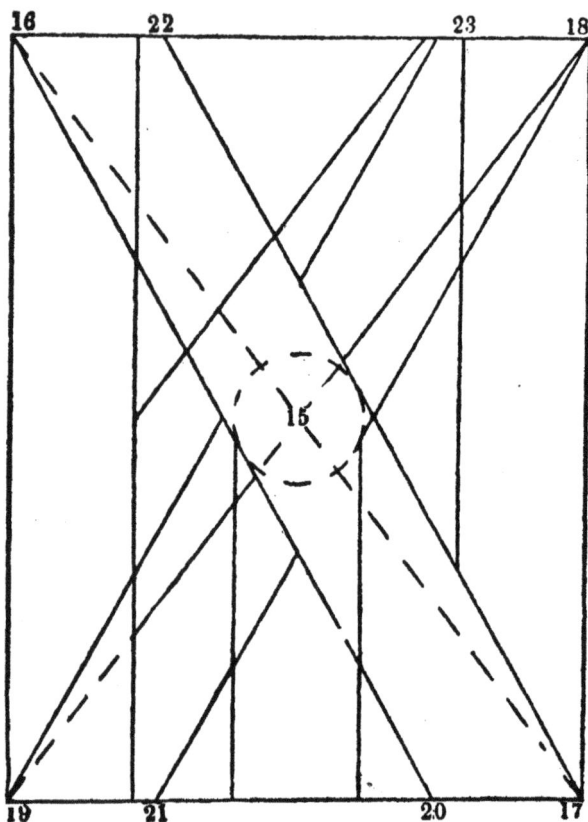

Fig. 27.—Monogram showing how to draw the letters
X, Y, N, and K.

Y is the upper half of X and the lower half of T
(Fig. 27).   Z (Fig. 26) is the upper and lower cross-bars
of E, and a slanting limb, drawn from top right to
bottom left, but not quite like the similarly-placed limb
of X in Fig. 27.   The centre round which the circle for
Z is drawn is found at the crossing of two lines (dashed
in the figure) from 13 to 14 and corresponding points.

Having found the centre and drawn the guide-circle, the leaning limb of Z is formed by drawing, from point 13, a line to touch the circle and pass on to the lower limb of Z, and then, from point 14, a similar line.

N (Fig. 27) is often a stumbling-block to the novice; and a common mistake he makes is that of drawing the leaning limb from top right to bottom left, instead of from top left to bottom right. To draw N, make the left and the right uprights, and between them the proper limb of X.

K (Fig. 27) is drawn by first making the left upright, then drawing the line 18, 19 from top right to bottom left corners, and another line parallel to it, at limb-width distance, towards the upper left corner. K is completed by adding the right-hand lower half of X.

Coming now to the rounded letters (Fig. 28), O is formed by drawing at top and bottom of the rectangle round the centres 32, 33, 34, and 35, four quarter-circles of radius equal to quarter-letter height added to half-limb-width. The dashed lines—24, 25; 26, 27; 28, 29; 30, 31—are all drawn at this distance from top, bottom, and sides respectively. Inside these four quarter-circles are drawn four others, smaller by a limb-width. These double quarter-circles are joined by the two middle portions of the right and left uprights of H and the two middle portions of the top and bottom cross-bars of E.

C is like O, except that the middle of the right up-right of H is not drawn and the ends of the quarter-circles are closed by the lines 36, 37 and 38, 39. G is like O with the bottom corner of the right upright of H added. Q is O with the end of A's right leaning limb added.

P is the left upright limb and portions of the top and the middle cross-bars of E. These portions of cross-bars are drawn after the curved parts. The curved parts are formed by half-circles drawn round the centre, 33. B is P with a second curved portion drawn below the top one, and like it exactly. D is B without the middle part of H's cross-bar and adjoining quarter-circles, and with the middle part of H's right upright.

J is the lower curved part of O, with the left end of the quarter-circle closed by the line 40, 41. This is joined to the upper part of the right upright of H.   U is J without a closed quarter-circle and the upper parts of both right and left uprights of H.

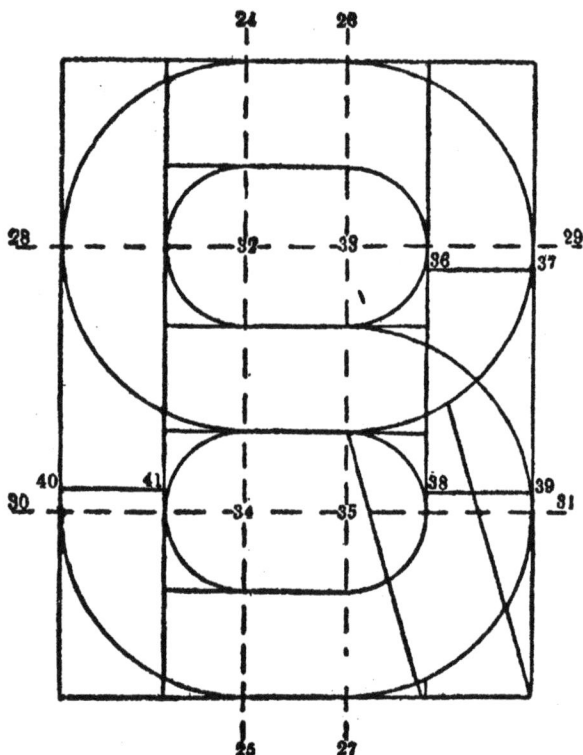

Fig. 28.—Monogram showing how to draw the letters
O. C, G, Q, P, B, D, J, U, R, and S.

R is P with the lower part of the right-hand portion of A added. R looks much better with a straight than a curved lower right limb. With R made this way, no difficulty will be felt ; but if a likeness is made between R's lower right part and B's, great difficulty will be found in making it look well.

S is the most difficult letter of all to form. It consists

of the upper part of C, the lower part of J, and two quarter-circles drawn round the centres 32 and 35, joined by the middle part of H's cross-bar.

In C, G, J, and S there are short lengths of upright limbs added to the ends of the quarter-circles before the cross-line is drawn closing them. In the monogram (Fig. 28) these short lengths are about quarter limb-width; but if a rule is wanted, they may be made

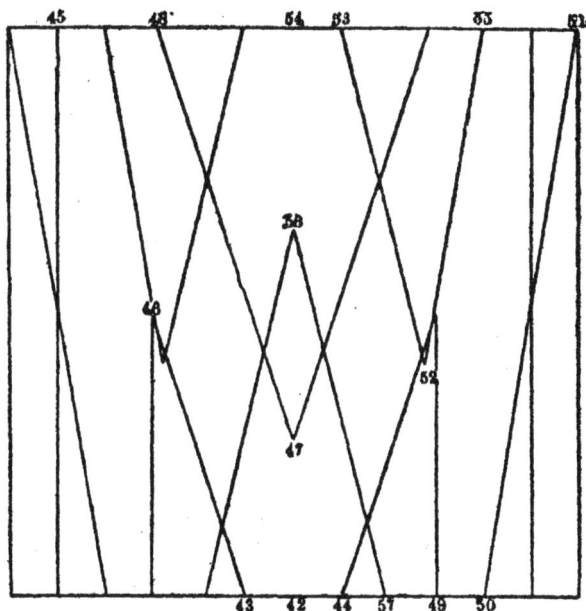

Fig. 29.—Monogram showing how to draw the letters M and W.

to extend one-third of the way towards the cross-bar of H, top or bottom, as the case may be.

M and W (Fig. 29) are drawn in rectangles of greater width than those enclosing the other letters of the same alphabet. These larger rectangles are, in the case of M, ten-ninths and, in the case of W, twelve-ninths of the usual width. In other words, the rectangle enclosing M must be wider than that enclosing A, B, or C, etc., by one-ninth; the rectangle enclosing W must be three-ninths wider than that enclosing A, B, or C, etc.

M is formed by drawing the right and the left uprights and adding the leaning limbs. Find 42, the middle point of the bottom of the rectangle, and on each side of 42 mark 43 and 44, so that the space between 43 and 44 is limb-width. Draw a line from 43 *towards* 45 as far only as 46 ; then draw a line from 47 to 48 parallel to 43, 46, and at limb-width distance from it. The other leaning limb is formed in the same way.

W is made by finding 49, one-fourth of the letter's width from right bottom corner. To the right of 49 mark 50, so that the space between 49 and 50 is equal to half limb-width. From 50 draw a line to 51, the top right corner. Draw 52, 55, a line parallel to 50, 51, at limb-width distance from it. Find 54, the middle point of the top of rectangle, and mark 53 half limb-width to the right of 54. From 53, towards 50, draw a line as far as 52 ; at limb-width distance from it, and parallel to it, draw 57, 56. The other two limbs of **W**—the left-hand side ones—are drawn in similar way.

The full-stop is a square placed on the line. It is of limb-width, and the same height. The comma is a full-stop with a tail, the diagonal half of a full-stop below the line. A colon is two full-stops, one above another, half limb-width apart. The semi-colon is a colon with a comma instead of a full-stop below. An apostrophe is a comma placed with the uppermost edge level with the tops of the letters. The same position is occupied by quotation marks. The quotation marks to the *left* of a word are commas upside down. The exclamation mark is a full-stop separated by half limb-width from part of an upright limb drawn above it. The hyphen is the cross-bar of **H**, separating two letters by letter-width.

The Arabic numerals cannot be said to have such definite proportions as block letters, neither can the hieroglyph &. However, One is represented by the letter I, Nought by the letter O, and the structure of the rest will be made out on carefully inspecting the numeral monogram (Fig. 30) on p. 31. Six is an inverted Nine. Eight is the foundation of the Six, Nine, Three and of the lower part of FIVE. The top part of FIVE is the cross-bar of the letter T. The upper half of the curved part of FIVE is unlike any part of the other figures. Two has its uppermost part shaped like THREE's and its lowermost part like L's. Its central part is formed by joining these two others, and is almost

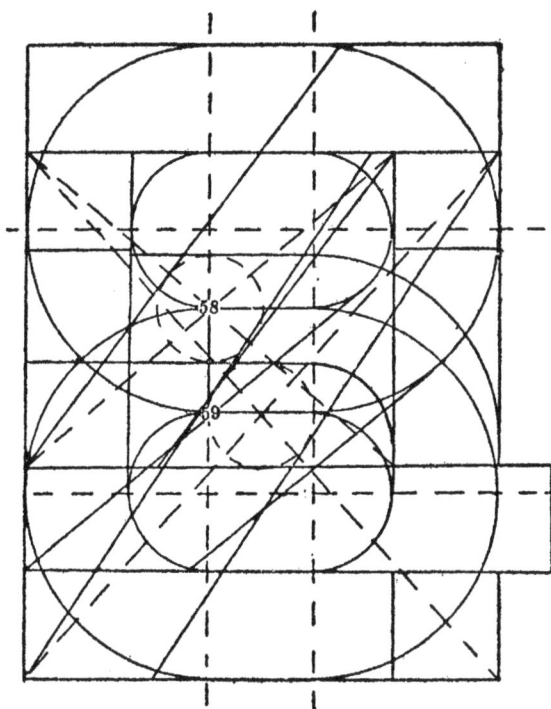

Fig. 30.—Monogram showing how to draw the Arabic numerals.

wholly a straight bar. SEVEN requires the whole of T's cross-bar, which is not bevelled off at the right-hand end. The leaning limb of SEVEN is formed in the same manner as the leaning limbs of X, Z, N, etc.—namely by finding the centre of the rectangle in which it is contained, and drawing the guide-circle round it. The lower line of the cross-limb of FOUR is raised one fourth of the letter-height, less half limb-width, above the bottom of the enclosing rectangle. The short projection to the right, beyond the upright limb of Four, is half the length of the short piece of the upright limb that comes below the cross-bar. Four is, therefore, that much wider than the rest of the figures.

Eight, which is the mother, so to speak, of many of the other figures, is drawn in the same way as S (Fig. 28) the part coming midway between top and bottom being, in the case of Eight, doubled and turned over. Three is the right-hand half of Eight, together with its upper and lower left-hand corners. The portion of H's cross-bar in Three's formation is drawn a little beyond the middle towards the left, before closing it with the line 58, 59 (Fig. 30, p. 31).

Six is the whole of Nought except the middle part of H's right limb ; to this is added the remaining part of Eight's lower loop. Nine is Six turned upside down. Briefly, Two, Three, Five, Six, Eight, Nine, and Nought, have all more or less of their forms in common, and One, Four, and Seven, are odd.

The hieroglyph & must be formed by drawing an Eight, and slightly altering it to bring out the two ends. Properly speaking, & is not to be formed mechanically.

Having written an alphabet, letter by letter, in the manner just described, it will be quite an easy matter to construct alphabets of other than plain block letters In course of time it will be found that wherever a few odd letters of some alphabet can be got, the rest can be added by building them up on the principle of the monogram alphabet here given.

It is necessary to repeat that whilst, for the learner's use a mechanical way of forming the letters by rule and compass is given, it must not for a moment be supposed that by such means ticket-writing, properly speaking, is done. The two parallels between which each line of letters is written are the only guides permissible, as soon as a sufficiently trained eye allows the rest to be dispensed with. Even these two lines will, in time, be found unnecessary ; such is the skill acquired by continuous and careful practice.

CHAPTER III.

THE SIGN-WRITER'S OUTFIT.

To do good work of any kind we require the best of tools, and the result of using bad tools is indifferent and unsatisfactory work. A description shall therefore now be given of the best and most durable tools required by the sign-writer, and also a few hints and directions as to their proper use and their care when lying idle. This latter point must always be attended to immediately the tools are done with, otherwise the pencils will soon become worthless for doing good work, besides causing an unnecessary outlay for new ones, and the apprentice or young workman should at the very commencement of his tuition take a pride in keeping in workmanlike condition and business order what will prove his best friends through life, perhaps his bread winner and his credentials, viz., his "kit of tools."

Under no circumstances is it advisable to purchase cheap and badly-made tools ; those of the best quality are the cheapest in the end, both as regards wear and tear and also the turning out of good work. This applies specially to camel-hair and sable pencils, and the colours and vehicles used in sign writing.

The reader who will follow the advice contained in this chapter will not have cause to complain of his tools, even though he may never become an excellent workman.

The hair pencils used by sign-writers are made in various sizes (which are distinguished according to the bird from which the quill was taken), see Figs. 31 to 43, and the student will do well to obtain a complete set as soon as he can afford it. He had better, however, commence with a few good pencils in preference to many common ones. The brush or pencil must be chosen according to the size or nature of the work in

Fig. 31.　　Fig. 32.　　Fig. 33. Fig. 34.　　Fig. 35.

Figs. 31 to 35.—Hair Pencils—large sizes.

hand; the small pencils being used for fine and delicate work, and the larger sizes for large lettering.

The goose, or full-goose size, would be a medium quill, and its cost would be : goose, about ninepence, and large goose fifteen pence. These two sizes, with a duck quill, costing about sixpence, would suit for almost anything up to six-inch work, using a flat long-hair fitch (Fig. 53) for filling in the letters. When buying, observe that the quill is well filled and the hair securely fastened.

Fig. 43.

Fig. 42.

Fig. 41.

Fig. 40.

Fig. 39.

Fig. 38.

Fig. 37.

Fig. 36.

Figs. 36 to 43.—Hair Pencils—small sizes.

The brush should taper to a fine point, and should maintain the point unbroken when in use. To test the brush, moisten it in the mouth, and then, whilst wet and the hair thus holding together, try the point by twisting it upon a finger nail making all sorts of circles and turns. If the point keeps firmly together, and the brush works with spring and solidity, it is a good article, but

Fig. 44.—Crow.

Fig. 45.—Duck.

Fig. 46.—Small Goose.

Fig. 47.—Goose.

Fig. 48.—Extra Goose.

Fig. 49.—Extra Small Swan.

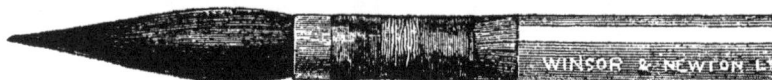

Fig. 50.—Small Swan.

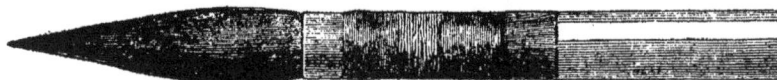

Fig. 51.—Middle Swan.

Fig. 52.—Large Swan.

Figs. 44 to 52.—Sable Pencils.

if the point splits and the hair spreads about, try another one.

The pencils are made in the sizes shown by Figs. 31

to 52 :—Crow, duck, small goose, goose, extra goose, extra small swan, small swan, middle swan, and large swan are the most useful sizes, and they will be found illustrated on page 36, Figs. 44 to 52.

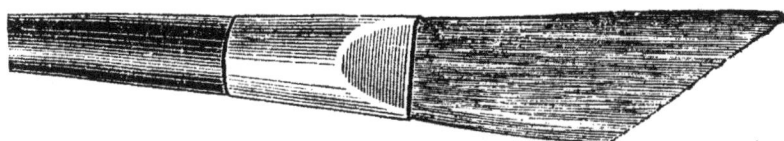

Fig. 53.—Long-hair Fitch.

Fig. 54.—Oval and Round Pencil Cases.

Camel-hair writers are the cheapest, and they are well-suited for some work, but with heavy paints they are useless, as the weight of the paint causes the brush

Fig. 55.—Crow.

Fig. 56.—Duck.

Fig. 57.—Small Goose.

Figs. 55, 56, 57.—Riggers.

to droop or sag, so that it is difficult to get a sharp, clear outline. Sable pencils (Figs. 44 to 52) are more expensive, but they are the best as the hair is stiffer than camel-hair, though just as pliable and considerably more durable. These must always be kept to perfection, and at once cleaned on the completion of a job. Another

Fig. 58.

Fig. 59.

Fig. 60.   Fig. 61.

Fig 62.

Fig. 63.

Fig. 64.

Figs. 58 to 64.—Sable Liners or Tracing Pencils.

class of pencil for writing, and so forth, is made from **brown ox hair; some call them "Taurus" pencils.**

They are not so fine as sable, but are considerably cheaper, and answer capitally for general use. Cleaning is best done by rinsing the pencils in turpentine, washing with soap and warm water, and dipping the points into sweet oil, finally putting away in a tin case (Figs. 54).

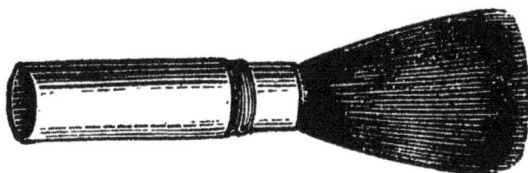

Fig. 65.—Short-hair or Filling-in Brush.

Fig. 66.—Filling-in Brush with Tin Ferrule.

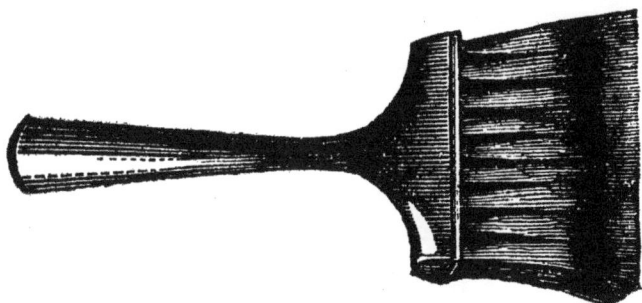

Fig. 67.—Badger-hair Softener.

Some workmen merely grease their brushes; for this purpose they have a little compartment in the tin box holding a supply of grease; others keep brushes always immersed in a little sweet oil at home. The best plan is to thoroughly clean them, as experience will teach. The wooden handles should be removed before putting the pencils away. A very good receptacle for the pencils is a long tin box which has contained wax vestas. The sixpenny size is the most useful, and as these may be bought without trouble, the young workman may soon possess as many as he requires.

The sign-writer will eventually also require "riggers,"

or short hair pencils (Figs. 55, 56, and 57), "liners"
(Figs. 58 to 64), and full, short hair or "filling-in"
brushes (Figs. 65 and 66). The use of these will be

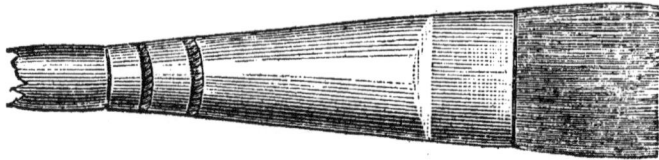

Fig. 68.—Sable Blender.

described in a future chapter. The badger-hair softener
(Fig. 67), is used for blending two or more colours on
any large surface, and the sable blender (Fig. 68) is used

Fig. 69.   Fig. 70.   Fig. 71.   Fig. 72.

Fig. 74.   Fig. 75.

Fig. 73.   Fig. 76.

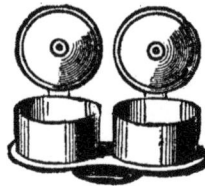

Fig. 77.   Fig. 78.   Fig. 79.

Figs. 69 to 79.—Tin Dippers.

for the same purpose in shading letters and blending their
colours.

Next come the wooden palettes, which are held in
the left hand, and are used for mixing and working the

colours upon. They are made in various shapes and sizes, as shown in Figs. 21—24 (p. 20). The last (Fig. 24) is a folding palette for the pocket, etc.

A few tin dippers are very useful appendages to these palettes. They are made with a flange clip for sliding on to the edge of the palette. Dippers are used for holding small quantities of tube colours, oils and

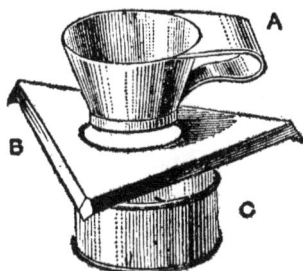

Fig. 80.—Paint Strainer.

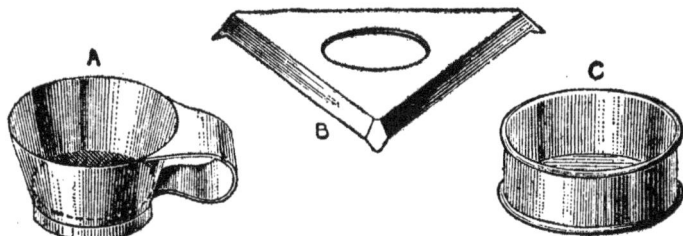

Fig. 81.—Parts of Paint Strainer : A, Strainer ; B, Stroddle ; C, Water Dish.

turps, so as to have them close at hand. A pair of tin dippers is illustrated on p. 21. Other forms are shown in Figs. 69 to 79.

A small paint strainer should be possessed by every sign-writer, and one of the most useful is that illustrated in Figs. 80 and 81. This strainer is designed to meet the wants of the sign-writing trade ; the triangle stroddle will rest over any sized paint pots, and there is a water dish for keeping the strainer in water when out of use. It is made of stout zinc, with brass wire gauze, and those who have used it say that it is

durable, easily kept clean, and cheap. The price for
the medium size is about 2s. 6d.

Fig. 82.

Fig. 83.

Fig. 84.

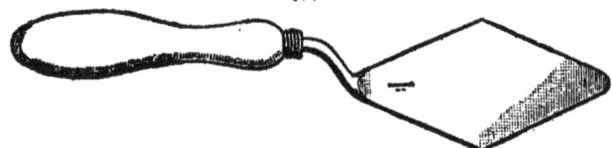

Fig. 85.

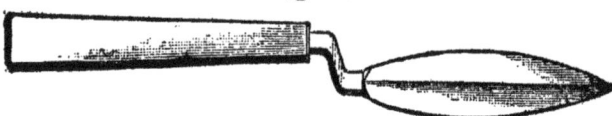

Fig. 86.

Figs. 82 to 86.—Palette Knives.

Fig. 87.—Compasses and Dividers.

Fig. 88.—Jointed Mahl or Rest Stick.

One or two palette knives (Figs. 82 to 86) will be
needed. Their price ranges from a shilling upwards. The

dividers (Fig. 87) are used for many purposes, such as measuring out spaces and describing· arcs, circles, ovals, and scrolls.

A useful and handy appliance for the sign-writer is the jointed mahl stick (Fig. 88). It is made in three or four divisions, and jointed after the manner of a fishing-rod, so that the stick can be made to any desired

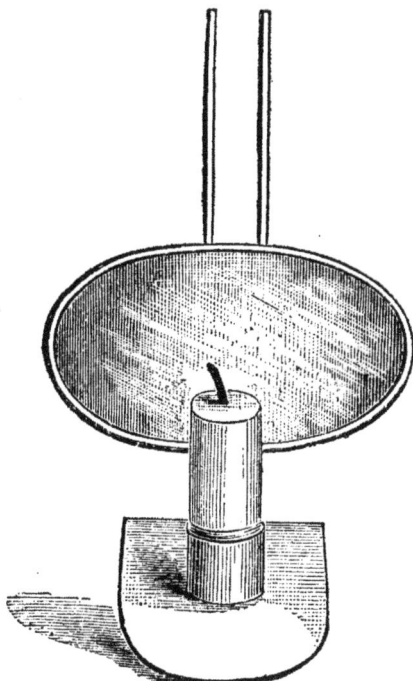

Fig. 89.—Sign-Writer's Candlestick with Shifting Reflector.

length according to the nature of the work. When taken to pieces it is conveniently carried.

The candlestick (Fig. 89) is furnished with a shifting reflector, so that the light can be thrown on any particular spot. It is also fitted with a flange clip for attaching to the palette. This is very useful when working awhile after sunset in order to complete a job, and for evening practice on the black board.

The young workman will also require some sticks of

pipe-clay, a chamois leather, a good sponge, cotton wool, and a chalk line and reel.

Brodie and Middleton's sign-writer's box (Fig. 90) is useful to every sign-writer. It is made of japanned tin, and to contain every requisite. There is a series of compartments, with tightly-fitting lids, to contain the paints, so avoiding the danger of their getting mixed and spoiled, as often accidentally happens when carried

Fig. 90.—Sign-Writer's Outfit in Japanned Tin Box

loosely in a basket. There are bottles, with screw lids, to contain oils, turpentine, varnishes, and other diluents ; spaces for gold leaf, brushes and pencils, and a palette. The spaces for the whole of these articles are so adjusted that there is a maximum of convenience with a minimum of bulk.

Scores of colours used by the sign-writer are enumerated in the full list of tube colours as put up by the artists' colourmen, but many of these colours are really hardly ever used by him. The following is a short list of those colours in request for the sign-writer's palette, and by mixing these a varied assortment of other tints and shades can be obtained :—Raw sienna, burnt sienna, raw umber, burnt umber, Vandyke brown, ultramarine, Prussian blue, indigo, yellow chrome (Nos. 1, 2, 3, 4), yellow ochre, ivory black, vegetable black, gamboge, yellow lake, green lake (Nos. 1, 2, 3, 4), emerald green, vermilion, Indian red, venetian red, crimson lake, scarlet lake, rose madder, flake white, white zinc.

A few other colours are best purchased in the dry state—in fact, they are not always found in the tube colour list. Amongst these are Chinese red, Persian red, orange lead, and they can frequently be made good use of, and often save some more expensive tube colours. This list refers to tube colours for lettering only, and not to those for painting the ground of sign-boards. Other colours can be bought in the dry state, but those most difficult to grind are purer and finer in tubes than those sold dry.

The novice need not purchase a full supply of the colours named in above list to commence with ; he may select a few most in accordance with his taste and requirements, and add others as wanted. There are four shades in chrome yellow and green lake respectively, but Nos. 1 and 3 will do to start with. Discretion and economy will prevent many halfpence being wasted on plant of no immediate use to its owner.

To excel in workmanship needs a thorough knowledge of the tools and of the materials to be manipulated. The sign-writer should have some idea of the bases and composition of the various pigments he works with, as unless the workman has some knowledge concerning the colours he uses, such as their liability to change or fade under certain conditions, their permanency, and the destructive qualities of some pigments when mixed with others, he cannot hope to execute permanent and satisfactory work This subject is one upon which whole books could be written, and its study would prove a great boon to the worker in paints.

House Decoration, a companion volume in this series of Handbooks, contains several chapters treating upon colour and paints, etc.

The general qualities of pigments, often called colours, are, on the authority of Mr. George Field, summarised as follows : (1) Beauty of colour, which includes purity, brightness, and depth ; (2) body ; (3) transparency or opacity : (4) working well ; (5) keeping in place ; (6) drying well ; and (7) durability. Few pigments possess all these qualities to an equal degree. Body, in opaque and white pigments, is the quality of efficiently covering surface , in transparent pigments it signifies richness of colour or tinting power. Working well depends much on sufficient grinding, or goodness of quality. Keeping in place and drying well depend greatly on the vehicles with which they are diluted or tempered. Durability also depends on the goodness of quality of both pigments and vehicles, and of the varnish used as the finishing coat. Bad varnish ruins a sign as quickly as bad oil and bad pigments, and is the most general cause of premature deterioration of work. This is a subject of which the sign-writer requires to have exceptional knowledge.

In the mixing of tints, great care and caution are necessary, not only to obtain a lasting colour, but also a bright and clear one, qualities which are often absent in home-made tinted colours. The ordinary painter fails as a tint manipulator, mostly because he uses wrong colours, and is not sufficiently clean in his methods, and does not allow the time necessary for proper and thorough mixing. Thus a pure, bright, clean tint seldom keeps so, but soon appears faded. But improper mixing, and insufficient blending of the pigments used, result in muddy, impure, and uneven tints. This will not do for the sign-writer, who must have bright, clean colours, or his work will prove a failure.

In mixing pigments, one great consideration is to get the tint, shade, or hue required with the least number of colours. Generally speaking, the less colours used in making a tint, the purer it is. But we must mix the proper colours necessary for the correct rendering of any tint according to the recognised formula. There may be more than one combination for obtaining most tints, and that which contains the least number of colours usually gives the best results.

White is the basis of all paints, and upon its virgin purity depends the resulting tint when the white is stained with colours. The best and *palest* linseed oil must be used for diluting and thinning : any other would spoil our work. The theory and practice in compounding paints is this. The very best white lead (or for indoor work, zinc white) is thinned down to a working consistency, or nearly so, and the requisite amount of driers is added. The paint must be well stirred, and left long enough—say half an hour—for the driers to incorporate with the oil, etc. The paint is next carefully strained, and the colours required for the tint are thinned with oil ; they should be measured in the required proportions, mixed together, and gradually added to the white, which must be constantly stirred until the desired tint is obtained. In this process there is some white paint to be transformed into some delicate tint, and to do this we dye it, or, as it is technically called, stain it. This is a proceeding somewhat different from taking certain portions of some two colours, such as red and yellow, and mixing them to obtain orange. Hence, certain transparent colours, as Prussian blue, siennas, and lakes, are " staining" colours used to obtain certain tints, by dyeing the basis of white paint to a tint required.

The sign-writer seldom has occasion to mix paints in large quantities, and he often mixes them on the palette, dipping the brush in the various colours, blending them on his palette, and then adding the white It is much better to take a little of each colour on the tip of a palette knife, wiping it clean of one colour before introducing to it the next, and then mixing with the knife or brush. The following selection of tints specially used by sign-writers is taken from the sign-writer's table of tints and shades :—

Buff.—Pale chrome yellow and white, tinged with a little Venetian red, or carnation, lake, and white.

Chocolate.—Vegetable black and Venetian red ; or white, Spanish brown, Venetian red, and vegetable black.

Claret.—Red, umber, and black.

Cream.—Chrome yellow, Venetian red, and much white.

Drab.—Raw or burnt umber and white, with a little Venetian red.

Fawn.—White and burnt sienna, ground very fine ; white, burnt umber, and Venetian red ; white, stone ochre, and vermilion.

Flesh Tint, Common.—Stain white lead with light red, and add a very little yellow ochre.

Flesh Tint, Fine. — White, lake, vermilion, and Naples yellow, or yellow ochre.

Gold. — White, stone ochre, and red ; pure light ochre ; white, yellow chrome, and burnt sienna to desired shade.

Green Tints.—White, Italian pink, Prussian blue ; Prussian blue, chrome yellow, and burnt umber (olive green) ; Prussian blue and yellow chrome (liable to fade) ; yellow ochre and indigo ; raw umber and indigo ; brown, pink, and indigo ; raw umber and Prussian blue (sage green) ; white and Brunswick green (pea green).

Grey Tints.—White and verditer, a blue hue ; white and indigo, a blue hue ; white, Indian red, and indigo, a brown hue ; white, light red, and Prussian blue, a brown hue ; white, burnt sienna, lake, and indigo, a brown hue.

Lead.—White, black, and indigo.

Lilac, Lavender, and French Greys.—White, lake, and indigo ; Indian red and Prussian blue ; white, indigo, and rose pink ; white, Prussian blue, and a little vermilion (French grey) ; white, with a little violet (lilac)

Peach.—Vermilion, Indian red, purple brown, and white ; white lead tinged with orpiment ; white, red, blue, and yellow.

Pearl Grey.—Prussian blue and black, equal portions, and white.

Pink.—White, vermilion, and lake; white, crimson lake, or scarlet lake.

Salmon.—White tinged with Venetian red; white tinged with vermilion; white tinged with yellow chrome, raw umber, and vermilion.

Silver.—White lead, indigo, and a little black, according to the shade required.

Snuff.—Vandyke brown and yellow.

Sky.—Prussian blue and white.

Straw.—White and pale chrome.

Violet.—Prussian blue, black, vermilion, and white; French ultramarine, white, and a little black.

This list will be found of service, but in some cases the worker may fail for a time in getting the desired tint, owing to wrong proportions in the various colours composing the tint. The exact proportions can only be found by repeated practical experiments. Experiment will show that the addition of any one colour gives the predominating tone of the tint, which also makes it warm or cold; by more white a lighter tint is produced, and more of all the darker colours gives a deeper shade. To understand this subject, the correct meanings of "tint," "shade," "hue," and "tone" must be remembered. The leading colour always gives the tone, which is the general effect as influenced by what are called warm or cold colours. Warm colours are those in which red or yellow predominate; and cold colours those in which blue and green tints appear. This subject is fully dealt with in HOUSE DECORATION.

Grey is termed the neutral tint, on account of it being the mean between black and white; but any two of the secondary colours will neutralise each other, as is the case with the primaries. The neutralising or compensating power is the foundation of all agreement or harmony amongst colours.

Contrast also requires much thought and study—this is the arrangement of colours, in such opposition or dissimilitude, that the one shall give greater visibility and effect to the other.

The arrangement of colours used for letters, and their harmony with the ground colour upon which they are painted, may be considered. Except in special cases where a certain colour is used as a sort of trade mark or distinguishing sign, the ground should not be a bright and glaring colour; but it should be a subdued and quiet tone. A ground of bright colour will not show up brilliant and showy writing so well as one of a quiet and neutral tone. Letters always stand out with greater distinctness on a quiet secondary or tertiary colour than they do on a primary colour, unmixed with white. On a neutral subdued ground letters are brought or thrown forward; on a bright gaudy ground they are lost, the greater prominence being given to the ground itself.

A great point in colouring a sign is to make its colours, as far as possible, emblematic, and suggestive of the business to which it relates. The style of lettering to be employed must also be chosen on the same lines, and it should be the effort of the writer to emblematise in every detail each sign he paints. The exact effect a given combination of colours will produce as a finished whole should be known. When we see a yellow or even a red letter on a black ground, we must always feel pity for that writer's taste.

It is a rule that one colour shall not overlap the one below it, so it is necessary to divide with a thin line the letter colour from the ground colour. Suppose green letters have been painted on a dark ground of reddish hue, such as purple brown, the harshness of the contrast is striking; then outline the letters with white or gold colour, and see how the effect is softened by this simple expedient. Or upon an emerald green ground paint letters with vermilion or Chinese red: the effect is worse than in the first case; but edge them with black or gold, and the effect is good. A black shading will throw the letters out, and help to give them a raised appearance. In some cases a coloured thickness may be rendered effective on a dark ground, the gold or white line being indispensable. It ought never to be allowed to impinge upon the colour of the letter

Colours for Lettering on Various Coloured Grounds.

	Ground Colour.	Letter Colour.	Shadows.
1	Stone colour	Black	White and dark stone colour
2	White	Any colour	Any colour
3	Black	White or gold	(Plain)
4	Light blue	Dark blue and vermilion	Light blue, dark shade, black, etc.
5	Bronze green	Gold, yellow, red	V e r m i l i o n, emerald green
6	Marble	White incised letters	—
7	Mahogany grain- ing	Any light colour and gold	Various
8	Walnut	Any light colour and gold	Various
9	Oak graining, dark	Gold or red	Dark colour and black
10	Oak graining, light	White	Black
11	Chocolate	Pink, salmon, fawn, primrose	Letter colours and black
12	Dark blue	Gold, outline white	Plain
13	Medium blue	Gold	Orange and Vandyke
14	Vermilion	Gold or yellow	Green, white, and black
15	Sage green	White	Purple brown and black

itself, unless that be of gold ; in which case it ought to be regarded not as a colour, but as the material which it represents. This principle was exemplified by Owen Jones in the interior decoration of the Great Exhibition of 1851. There the primary colours were so arranged as to neutralise each other ; and to avoid harsh antagonism from their contact, or any undesired complementary secondaries arising from their immediate proximity, a line of white was interposed between them, which had the effect of softening and giving them their true colour value. These remarks do not apply to letters on a black ground. The edging round the letters must be boldly and neatly done, especially on gilded work, with the best sable pencils ; it must show no sign of timidness or indecision, otherwise the line will have a rough, ragged appearance, and completely spoil the letters. Gold letters particularly show up an unequal line:

It may require some time for the student to find out which coloured letters look best on certain coloured grounds ; but he need only take a walk along the streets to see hundreds of practical examples. The table given on page 51 shows quite a wide range of useful combinations, and each item is numbered for possible future reference.

The preceding table is a short list, and refers mainly to simple plain lettering. It is inserted for the special purpose of giving assistance to the beginner who has no knowledge of the subject. The learner should now be able, from the directions given, to proceed with the practical application of colours with some degree of success.

CHAPTER IV.

MAKING SIGNBOARDS AND LAYING GROUND COLOURS

THE making of signboards is carpenter's work, but the sign-writer should give proper instructions to the carpenter in order to ensure a suitable article being made. Some simple directions as to making a sign-board, and painting and preparing the surface ready for receiving the sign-writer's inscription thereon are therefore given here.

The wood used in the manufacture of signboards must be well-seasoned and perfectly dry when being worked, and it should be as far as possible free from knots; the only effectual cure for these is to cut them out and insert a piece of sound wood. Not every kind of wood is suitable for this purpose. For instance, if the board were of pitch-pine, the paint would not remain on it if it were exposed to the sun. The resin would liquefy and push off the paint, especially if this were black. The best wood, commonly used for signboards, is good old yellow pine, and next comes any old, dead, well-seasoned white-wood. In any case, wood that contains sap must be avoided. The expensiveness of mahogany stands in the way of its general adoption, otherwise this is far superior, and a well-made sign-board of Honduras mahogany will serve for generations.

A signboard should contain as few joints as possible, so it is advisable to use wide boards in its construction. The thickness of the board often varies according to the size of the sign, and opinions appear to differ considerably on the point. One who has been making and painting and writing signboards for fifty years, considers that ½ in. to ¾ in. stuff is quite thick enough, and that when properly made the thinner they are the better.

A carpenter would make a cheap and serviceable sign-board, as shown in Fig. 91. He would employ a frame the size required, dovetailed at the corners, as at A, having a width equal to or greater than that of the proposed board and a depth about three times its width. To make a frame for a panel, c, of 1 in. stuff,

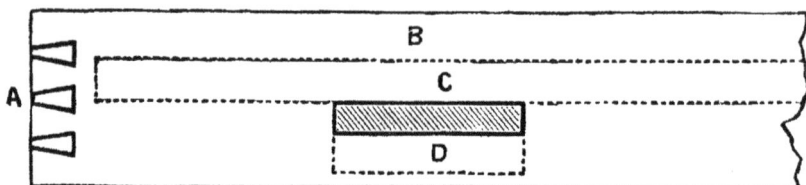

Fig. 91.—Making Frame for Signboard.

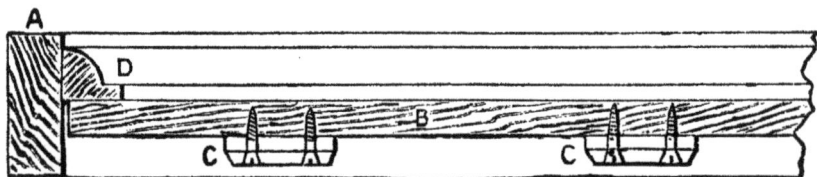

Fig. 92.—Section of Signboard.

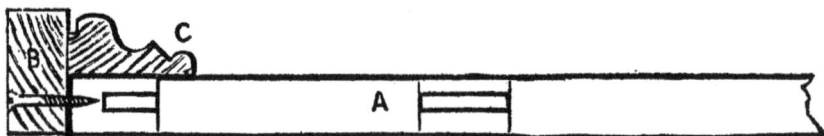

Fig. 93.—Covered Signboard.

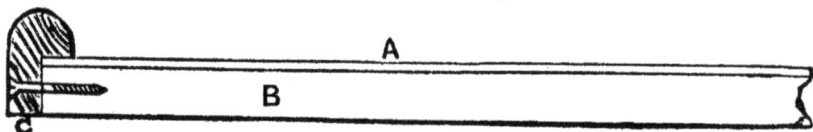

Fig. 94.—Glazed Signboard.

use strips $3\frac{1}{2}$ in. by 1 in., or $1\frac{1}{4}$ in., with dovetailed joints at the corners; the ends of the ledges, D, which cross the board, should fit into mortises in the frame as shown in Fig. 91. To avoid weakening the frame excessively, these mortises should be nearly central, with tenon shouldered behind the ledge. The panel itself should fit easily in the frame, and be screwed from the back through holes in the ledges, all the holes except those in the centre being elongated to allow a trifling movement when the boards which form the panel shrink or expand.

The end-grain of the panel boards must be well painted before fixing, then a moulding can be fitted in the angle formed by the face of the panel board and the inner edge of the frame. This moulding is fixed to the frame and not to the board, which ensures a durable and an economical construction.

A prepared canvas is made in very large sizes by floor-cloth manufacturers and is used for the purpose of covering gigantic signboards. This canvas stands well when the frame has enough ribs to prevent the canvas vibrating under the influence of wind. Frames for these large canvas signs should be made of yellow deal timber from $3\frac{1}{2}$ in. to $4\frac{1}{2}$ in. wide, and $1\frac{1}{2}$ in. to 2 in. thick. These should be framed together by mortise and tenon like a door without panels, and painted well before canvas is put on. Moulding is applied either by rebating or screwing to the edge of frame.

The heart side of a board is the best for the face side of a sign, but the carpenter will prepare the reverse side if not specially instructed, as the outer-side is easier to plane smooth. Particularly should the heart side be used for the face when prepared canvas is fixed upon the wood like a veneer. This is an excellent plan for making curved signs.

Frames for glass signs may be made like Fig. 92, but preferably with a moulding like Fig. 93. Upon the wooden back, behind a glass facia, there should be a soft cloth or felt, to prevent injury to the painting and gilding at the back, and special care should be taken to prevent the entrance of water.

Another way to make a signboard is to place battens about 3 ft. apart; rebate their edges and fix with buttons screwed, not too tightly, to the board. This will allow it to expand and contract, the battens being left a trifle shorter than the width of board, so that the cappings will not be pushed off on the board contracting.

The caps, mouldings, etc., may be put on by any skilled woodworker.. In jointing a signboard never use glue, but in its place use paint. Instead of groove and tongue some prefer a smooth, straight slot joint with iron dowels. All battens, mouldings, caps, etc., should be well painted before being put together; all external woodwork should be jointed with paint. Glue is a source of great trouble when used; its affinity for moisture keeps the parts wet, and causes rot and decay in external woodwork.

For general work the boards are planed smooth and true, and tongued and grooved in dovetailed manner, the better to prevent them opening. The boards are laid, edge to edge, close together face downwards upon some level surface, and ledges or cross pieces, not to be more than two feet six inches apart, are firmly attached to the back with plenty of strong screws.

To clamp up the boards before having the cross pieces affixed would be a great mistake, because signboards are exposed to all weathers, hot and cold, wet and dry, consequently they undergo a large amount of expansion and contraction. When the boards are clamped up, which is frequently done, allowance is not made for their expansion, so in wet or damp weather, when the boards expand and exert a tremendous force, this causes the whole signboard to warp and twist. Dry weather will cause the boards to shrink and leave glaring cracks at the joints. When making a signboard the carpenter should therefore use his skill and knowledge to overcome this swelling and shrinking. The science of making signboards is to do away with all these defects.

An ornamental moulding placed around a signboard should be mitred at the corners, and placed as in a picture frame; it should be screwed to the edges of the frame, and never to the front of the signboard.

A carpenter who makes signboards a specialty, can generally be relied upon to turn out a good article without receiving special instructions. These hints will, however, assist the young sign-writer to give special orders to a carpenter ; and these should be written in the form of a specification, in order to avoid disputes. Bad work, which shows itself in cracked, warped, and twisted signboards, such as one may sometimes discover, renders abortive the labour and art bestowed upon them by the painstaking sign-writer.

The preparation of the surface for lettering, when the carpenter has delivered the board properly glass-papered and perfectly smooth, is a job generally done by the ordinary house-painter, or beginner, and when they do the work in their own way, without special instructions it often happens at sign-writing that soon after completion the signboard blisters, the colour fades or the paint cracks. The clever sign-writer who is fully employed, cannot afford to do this preparatory work himself, but he should have it done under his immediate supervision, for his reputation rests upon the lasting result of the sign he paints ; and it behoves him therefore, to see that great care is taken in preparing the groundwork of his signboards.

Some firms employ men who thoroughly under-stand the whole process of preparing the ground, and in such cases the sign-writer need give himself no trouble.

The many ways of preparing signboards have their advocates and detractors alike. But no matter which method may be adopted, when there are any knots in the wood the first process is to effectually destroy the damaging power of these, carefully coating them with patent knotting. When this has dried the knots are glass-papered, and again carefully coated. The panel is now ready to be primed with equal proportions of red and white lead, to which raw linseed oil, a little driers, and a little turpentine may be added ; this priming should be thoroughly strained. When this is perfectly dry, a second coat of the same priming may be put on, but both must be laid very thinly and sparingly, especially if the panel is made of oak or mahogany. This priming must be allowed to get quite dry and hard, and then it may be rubbed down with glass-paper.

The signboard now receives a thin coat of the ground colour, mixed in the ordinary way; it is allowed to get dry and hard, and is then glass-papered. The processes are repeated, but this time the glass-papering is done with extra care. Next a good round coat of flatting of the same colour is laid, and if this does not sufficiently cover the board, it must be lightly rubbed down with fine glass-paper and again flatted. Now it must be decided whether the panel is to be varnished before or after lettering; if the former, it receives two good coats of copal or amber varnish; if the latter, it is ready for the sign-writer without any further work.

Another method of preparing the ground is as follows. The back and front of the signboard are brushed over with equal quantities of linseed oil, japanner's gold size, and turpentine, to which a little ground white lead is added, rubbing the material well in. The second coat is composed of equal quantities of white lead, common spruce ochre, and whiting, all well dried and ground fine and stiff, separately, with raw oil. The whole are mixed and sufficient gold size is added to cause the mixture to dry quickly, firm, and hard; turpentine is added to make it of proper consistency, and two or three coats are then applied to the board. When dry and hard the surface is rubbed smooth with sand paper or pumice stone and water. Equal portions of spruce ochre, whiting, bath brick, and white lead are ground with two parts oil and one part turpentine, a little gold size diluted with turpentine is added and one, two, or three coats are applied as may be necessary, the panel being rubbed down and washed off between each coat. Repeat the rubbing and colouring until the surface is smooth and level like plate glass, and it is then fit to receive the final coat upon which to write, marble, or grain.

Whether it be a plain ground, landscape, figures, or letters, the finishing coat ought to stand until thoroughly dry and hard. The signboard should be finally varnished twice with best body copal or amber varnish, as the delicacy of the painting demands.

For temporary purposes, signboards may be prepared with a coat of size, or, better still, with ordinary distemper, that is, size and whiting, and when dry, the surface should be rubbed down with fine glass-paper and the boards well dusted.

American cloth or leather is a material frequently used as a surface for the sign-writer to work upon for temporary purposes, such as bazaar or fancy fair announcements. In such cases the cloth may be simply stretched on a frame, and the letters painted direct upon the black shining surface. This is a simple expedient as a cheap substitute for a wooden signboard.

For covering signboards that are very dilapidated, and when the expense of a new board is not allowable, the face of the signboard may be covered with stout American cloth, made to adhere to the board with bootmaker's paste, which is made of glue, flour, and alum. The cloth must be large enough to lap over the edges of the board, and must be closely tacked down all round with *tinned* tacks ; iron or blue tacks rust and soon rot the fabric. The cloth, if well pasted, should dry out perfectly taut and free from wrinkles.

As a preservative, the edges of the board, where the tacks are, are painted with a good coat of red and white lead mixed thick, taking care to keep the front of the cloth surface clean. The mouldings, which have been primed and given one coat of paint, are next bradded on, and nail-holes, joints, etc., well stopped with putty. The back of the board and the mouldings next receive three good coats of slate colour paint made with black, white lead and red lead.

The surface of the cloth itself being shiny and non-porous requires but two thin coats of paint, mixed with equal quantities of copal varnish, raw linseed oil, and turpentine. The first coat must be allowed to get perfectly hard, when it is lightly glass-papered with No. 0 or No. 1, and is then ready for the second coat. If the writing is to be put on before varnishing, the surface should be flatted in the same colour as that used for the first coats. When this is thoroughly hard, it is ready for the lettering to be set out. For binding on the flatting copal varnish should be used, and also for finishing off the signboard.

Canvas will be found to answer every purpose for large pieces to be set up out of doors, whilst for small indoor pieces holland will do. The canvas may be bought ready tanned, or this can be done by soaking it in tanning liquor for forty-eight hours. The tanning liquor is made by boiling 2½ lbs. of good oak tan in 4½ gals. of soft water for thirty minutes. Stretch the canvas on its frame, and then paint the writing surface evenly with several coats of good oil paint till a smoothish surface is obtained. If a very smooth surface is needed, it can he glass-papered or pumice-stoned between the application of successive coats. A flat board is placed so that it supports the canvas from behind whilst this is being done.

When writing a fresh inscription upon an old signboard, it is frequently necessary to clean off all the old material and otherwise prepare it, to make it fit for repainting. The old paint can be burnt off with the spirit torch, and the board rubbed smooth with sharp new glass-paper. Holes, cracks, and other imperfections should next be stopped with white lead and putty, and the knots freshly coated with knotting. The board should be primed with equal parts of red and white lead mixed with oil and turps. This priming has great protecting power, and soon dries quite hard. The oxides of iron and the earths have little body, and are consequently unfitted for the purpose.

Much might here be said as to the general tints and shades of colour which show off the lettering to the best advantage, but a great deal must be left to individual taste and requirement. Gold lettering is always most effective upon a black groundwork ; the letters show up plainly, viewed from any angle: this is not so with a white or other light ground. Gold letters also look well on a groundwork of dark blue, or of bronze green, when properly shaded. Gold also shows up well on a ground of Chinese red, the colour used on the Royal Mail carts. It is liable to fade when exposed to the light and weather, so several coats of flatting must be applied, and after the gold leaf has been affixed, it must be protected with two good coats of varnish. A black letter shows up best on a white ground, but a white letter on a black ground is much more effective. This is particularly so with small lettering on a limited space containing much matter. Boards crowded with lettering can be read easiest and at a greater distance when the letters are white on a black ground, using oxide of zinc or, better still, Charlton white, but never white lead. When tube paint is used, flake white is good ; this is the carbonate of lead which does not discolour so quickly on exposure to the atmosphere.

There is another species of ground, the marbled or grained surface, frequently seen on shop facias ; an inscription written on this in the ordinary style generally looks bad. It frequently appears as though the grain of the wood or veins of the marble spring out in all directions from the letters themselves. A grained ground is unsuitable and the employment of a tablet painted in one colour, which harmonises with the graining colour around it is preferable. If a grained ground is used, it should imitate a material very different from that used for the rest of the work, and should contain a small close grain.

Only one class of letter looks really well written on an imitation marble surface; that is the imitation incised letter. It is difficult to write, and requires skilful handling to look effective and real. If the whole of a shop front is marbled, and the lettering has to be inscribed also on a marble surface, the facia or signboard which is to receive the writing should be painted a marble of a lighter tone, which gives it the appearance of a slab let into the main surface.

CHAPTER V.

THE SIMPLER FORMS OF LETTERING.

IN previous chapters, freehand and other methods of drawing have been considered in a general way, but attention must now be given to the best course to pursue in order to become proficient in accurately forming and drawing the letters of the alphabet without mechanical aid. Directions shall be given later for making various guide lines, which are sometimes used by the sign-writer as an aid in forming accurately and quickly some of the more difficult characters, such as C, G, S, and &. The student must, however, first be able to draw in a bold and workmanlike manner by freehand alone, using only his eye as his guide. Guide lines may be very good in their place, but the young student who wishes to master this art and become a capable workman must eschew them altogether in the preliminary stages of practice. The best writers do not make use of these aids to correct drawing; they trust to the eye and hand alone, and the best display and bold work, which invariably bears the imprint of the master hand and the artistic eye and mind, is done in this way.

Occasionally it is next to impossible to construct letters correctly without the help of mechanical means, as, for instance, when the workman is confined in a very awkward and cramped position, or is up aloft on a frail platform, and at a height sufficient to unsteady the nerves and, consequently, the hand. Again, supposing very large letters have to be painted on the wall of a house, also at a great height; it is almost impossible for the workman to have sufficient space to stand away far enough to occasionally survey his work, and judge of its appearance or detect any imperfections of letters. In such circumstances as these the use of any mechanical aid or guiding lines is perfectly legitimate.

The most dexterous and expert sign-writers seldom chalk out their letters, but write them in offhand with the brush and colour. Even when they previously mark out their letters, it is in a rough and sketchy manner, chiefly with the object of properly spacing the letters and evenly filling in the allotted space on the board. They very seldom follow the chalk lines when painting the letters.

In commencing to draw the alphabet in freehand, it is better for the learner to practice with simple fine line letters, such as those "skeleton" letters, together with numerals, given in Figs. 95, 96, and 97.

In the first place, these should be drawn on paper with the lead pencil, for practice; but when the learner has practised this hard and attained some success, recourse should be had to the blackboard, and the drawing should be done with both the chalk and the camel-hair pencil filled with colour. It takes but very few words to describe the method of procedure for a first attempt upon the alphabet, but it is the foundation of letter-forming and letter-painting. It is very important that the student should completely master this, because he must be able to form each letter in, at least, a creditable style before he can hope to be reckoned a craftsman and earn money by his craft. Therefore, at this stage of the beginner's work, even more than at any other, there must be continual practice.

Failures there must and will be at the commencement, but repeated practice will surely, if slowly, overcome all difficulties.

Some letters will be most difficult to form correctly, especially the S and the "short and"—&; but each succeeding effort will produce some improvement, however slight and imperceptible to the untrained eye. As the work improves in quality, the workman will be

ABC
DEF
GHIJ
KLM

Fig. 95.—Skeleton Letters.

NOP
QRS
TUV
WXY

Fig. 96.—Skeleton Letters,

Fig. 97.—Skeleton Letters and Numerals.

better able to see its imperfections, although, perhaps, he cannot tell exactly where the faults lie. But afterwards he will perceive and locate these also, and eventually be able to correct bad lines, with a precise and masterly touch. When he has surmounted the somewhat difficult task of forming in shapely and pleasing manner all the letters which our alphabet contains, his great obstacle on the road to progress is passed. Progress

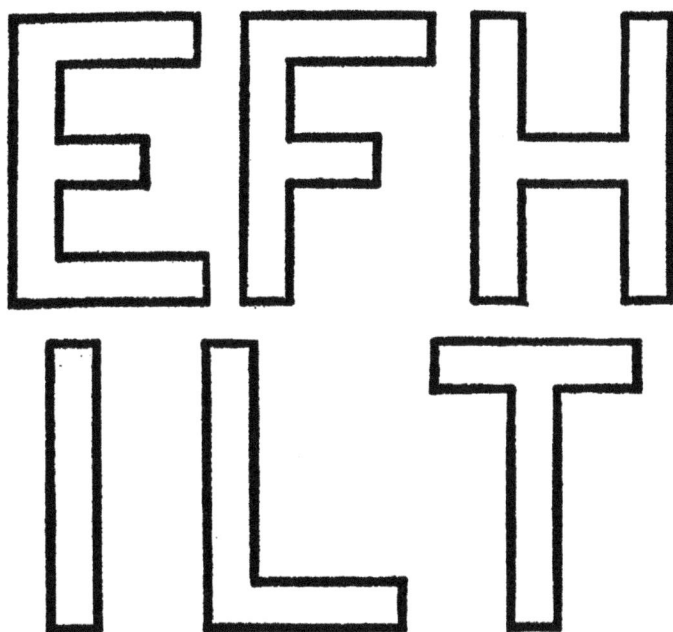

Fig. 98.—Letters Formed of Straight Lines at Right Angles.

will follow naturally and easily to him, with one possible exception—that of colours and colouring.

The examples given in the accompanying skeleton alphabet on pages 64 to 66 should be drawn on a larger scale, as should also the other freehand exercises that are given on several other pages.

Let us now consider the letters of the alphabet as they stand in relation to the sign-writer and his work. They are here grouped into five divisions, for the sake of clearness and the proper understanding of the subject.

It will be readily understood the easiest letters to form are those which consist wholly of parallel lines at right angles to each other. The letters in this group are shown in Fig. 98. This drawing shows the sans-seriff order of letter, which are given here in outline only. In forming letters, no precise rule can be followed as to their general construction and symmetry, Letters may be of an average width and length, or they may be "elongated" or "extended," and consequently the distances between all parallel lines vary accordingly. Referring to Fig. 98 and the letters E and F, the middle

Fig. 99.—Letters Formed by Oblique Lines.

members (which expression indicates each portion of which the letter is "built up") should never be quite so long as the outside ones. They may be nearly so, but should never be less than one half as long as the other members. The letter H has one horizontal member exactly in the middle of the two uprights. This should be of the same width or thickness as the rest of the letter.

The other three letters are some of the easiest to form, and require no remarks other than that the top member of the T should always be equally distributed on each side of the upright.

The group Fig. 99 shows the only letters which are composed wholly of slanting or oblique lines. The V is not difficult to form if care be taken not to give it an appearance of falling or leaning on either side, but to allow each arm or member to slant at the same angle. W resembles two V's joined together, but must not be so wide, or it will give a very unsightly appearance to the whole word of which it is a part. For letters of normal dimensions, the average width of the W should be about half as wide again as the letters F or N ; elongated and extended letters are not at present under consideration. The X is generally formed in a rectangle, and the upper

Fig. 100.—Letters Formed by Combined Vertical, Horizontal, and Oblique Lines.

triangle, formed by the members crossing, should be very slightly smaller than the lower one. The lower portion must never be the smaller of the two, or the letter will look ugly and top-heavy.

Another group is the letters formed of combined vertical, horizontal, and oblique lines shown in Fig. 100. A is simply an inverted V with the addition of a cross member, which should be nearer the bottom than the top, as shown in the drawing. It is somewhat difficult to draw **K** to give it a pretty appearance.   The style shown here is that generally accepted, at least for all plain lettering.   **M** is a wider letter than **N**, but the middle member should not be shortened, as is sometimes done, it should be allowed to come down to the base line. Some writers have likened **M** to **V**, supported on each side by perpendiculars, the lines of the **V** starting from

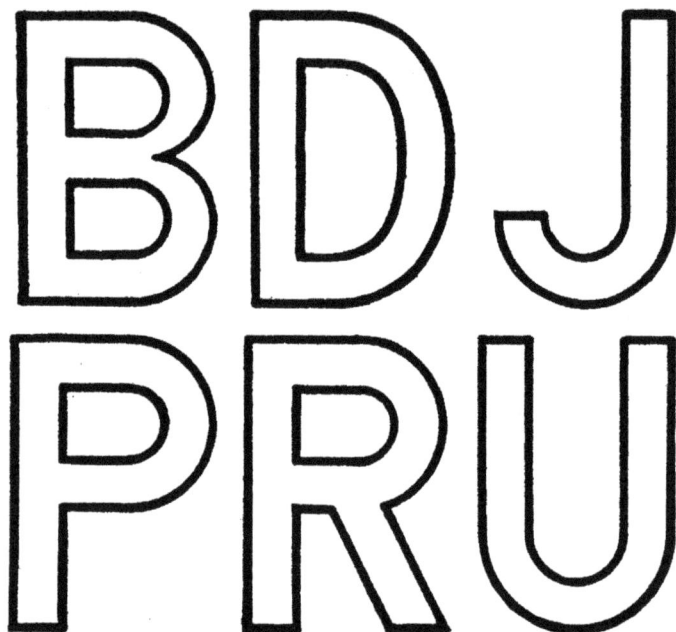

Fig. 101.—Letters Formed by Combined Straight and Curved Lines.

about the centre of the top of the vertical members. This is a very good description of the letter **M**.   The way to draw **N** is to draw the perpendicular lines of equal width, and the oblique one from the inner angles **Y** is fashioned after a **V**, supported on a single stem, and **Z** is formed within a rectangle.

The next group is letters composed of both straight and curved lines (Fig. 101.)   The construction of **B** and **R** are very similar, the only difference being in the lower member, which in **B** curves inwards and in, **R** curves out-

wards, though, as explained on p. 28, a good appearance
is more easily obtained if the lower limb of **R** be made
perfectly straight. The lower curve in **B** should always
be slightly fuller than the upper one ; the letter is thus
saved from having a top-heavy appearance, and looks
altogether more solid. The **D** consists of a perpendicular
and a full-length curve, the **P** of a perpendicular and a
half-length curve, the **J** a perpendicular with a curved

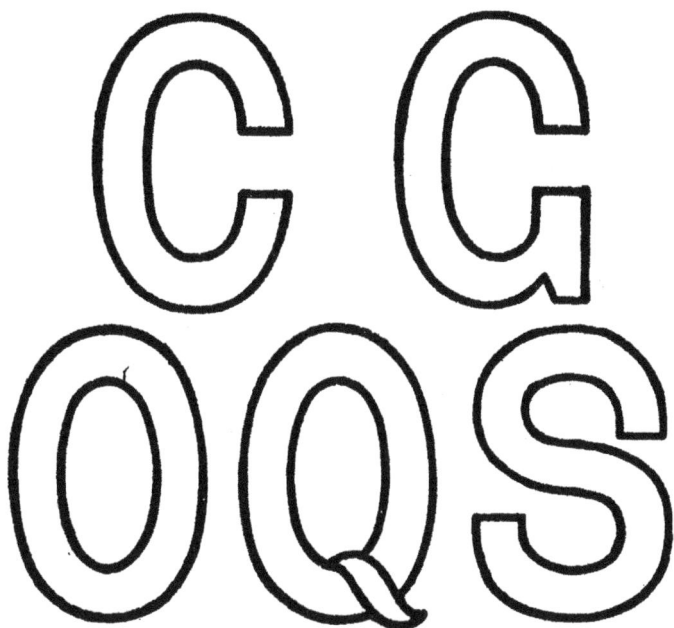

Fig. 102.—Letters Formed Chiefly by Curved Lines.

base, and the **U** a curved base continued into two
perpendiculars.

The group that now remains (Fig. 102) contains the
five most difficult letters, which consist entirely of curved
lines, and it is the foundation upon which **C**, **G**, and **Q**
are constructed. **O** should be a perfect ellipse. **S** is the
most difficult letter for a novice to draw, but by assidu-
ously practising freehand drawing he should soon be
able to give it a graceful rendering without any
extraneous aid. The letter should be contained within
a parallelogram, and it should have a proportionate

appearance throughout. If the learner wishes he can adopt
certain guide-lines for the correct drawing of this letter,
but it is not recommended, for if the eye is not trained
to a correct perception and an accurate discrimination,
and if the hand has not, as the result of experience, the
power of exact definition and precise demonstration, the
ultimate result will be indefinite and unsatisfactory.

In Chapter II. the method of forming each letter
of the alphabet by mechanical means has been fully
explained, but, as there pointed out, such a method
would not be adopted by the practical sign-writer. It
has been thought advisable therefore in this chapter, even
at the risk of some repetition, to explain how each letter
is formed and point out its relation to other letters without any reference to mechanical ways of drawing letters.

Having learnt that all letters are formed of lines
straight and curved, either singly or combined, the
student should now be better able to understand the
individual construction and character of all letters in
our alphabet. But it is necessary to consider the alphabet of small letters, called by the printing profession
"lower case." They may be divided into four classes,
short, ascending, descending, and "kerned" letters. The
short letters are a, c, e, i, m, n, o, r, s, u v, w, x, z; ascending letters are b, d, f, h, k, l; and descending letters are
g, j, p, q, y. "Kerned" letters are those which have part
of their face overhanging either one or both sides of
their shank. In the Roman type f and j are the only
"kerned" letters, but in Italic *b, d, f, g, h, j, k, l, p, y*
are kerned. "Kerned" letters are so made by type
founders, because the compositor has no share in the
proper spacing of letters; the sign-writer, however, has
unrestricted freedom in the spacing of his letters and
displaying his words. It is to this point that the fore-
going analysis of the alphabet has been leading. Where
the novice is using kerned letters he must give special
care and attention to their spacing, otherwise his completed work may have an ungainly and awkward
appearance.

To make this apparent, suppose the sign-writer is called upon to write in Italic letters the word

S|w|a|f|f|h|a|m

and he spreads the letters as here shown ; the word looks most unsatisfactory—divided in the middle as much as if it consisted of two words. This is caused solely by bad spacing. Now let us see how the same word appears when judiciously spaced, as in this specimen—

Swaffham

The word has now a symmetrical appearance. In the first example the fact that the "kerned" letters take up more space in width than the others causes the unsightly spacing ; so, to have each letter symmetrically spaced in this particular word, it is necessary to have the short letters a little farther apart than they would be if no "kerned" letters were used. Words such as this require much forethought, but the subject of spacing will be dealt with fully in a subsequent chapter. Enough has been said to show that it is essential to consider the alphabet in all forms and combinations, for such knowledge will be most important in after-work.

It is necessary to give this minute analysis of the alphabet, as all good sign-writers should possess such knowledge. Most of the various styles of letters used by sign-writers are more or less close copies of ordinary printing type letter. This probably results from the sign-writer originally learning his letter forms from the specimens of letters found in "Books of Alphabets," which are frequently printed from ordinary type. Many professionals make complete sets of ornamental letters from any printed example which takes their eye, but without much regard for artistic effect.

A B

C D

E F

Fig. 103.—Roman Capitals, Solid.

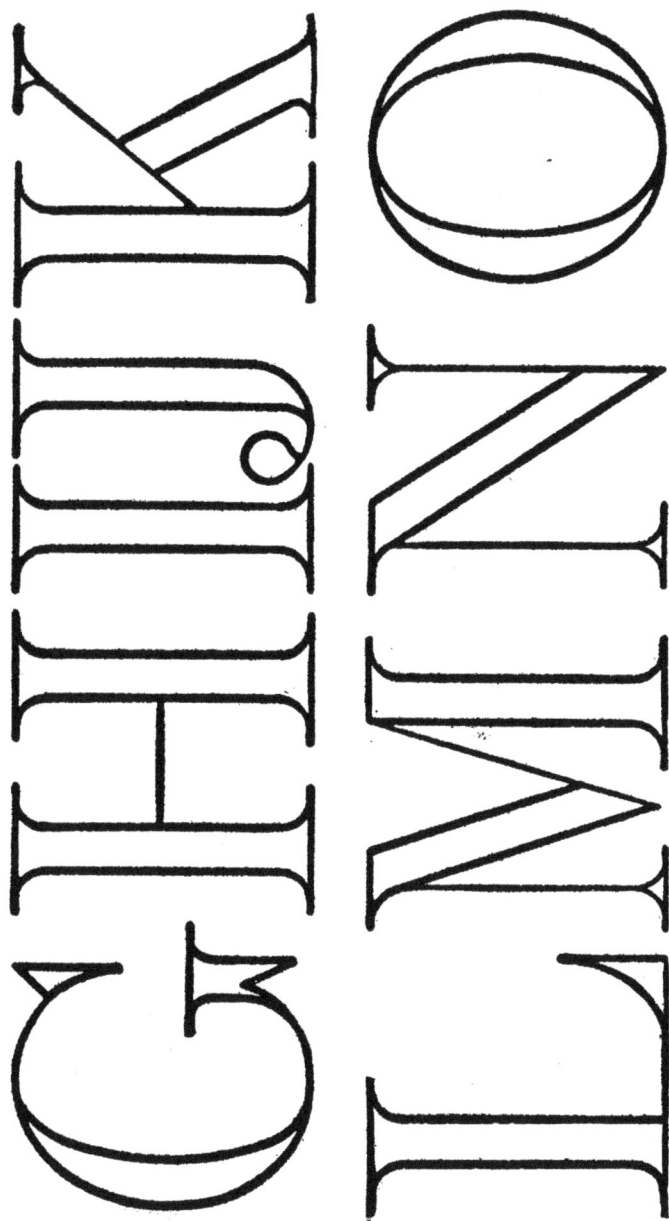

Fig. 104.—Roman Capitals, Open.

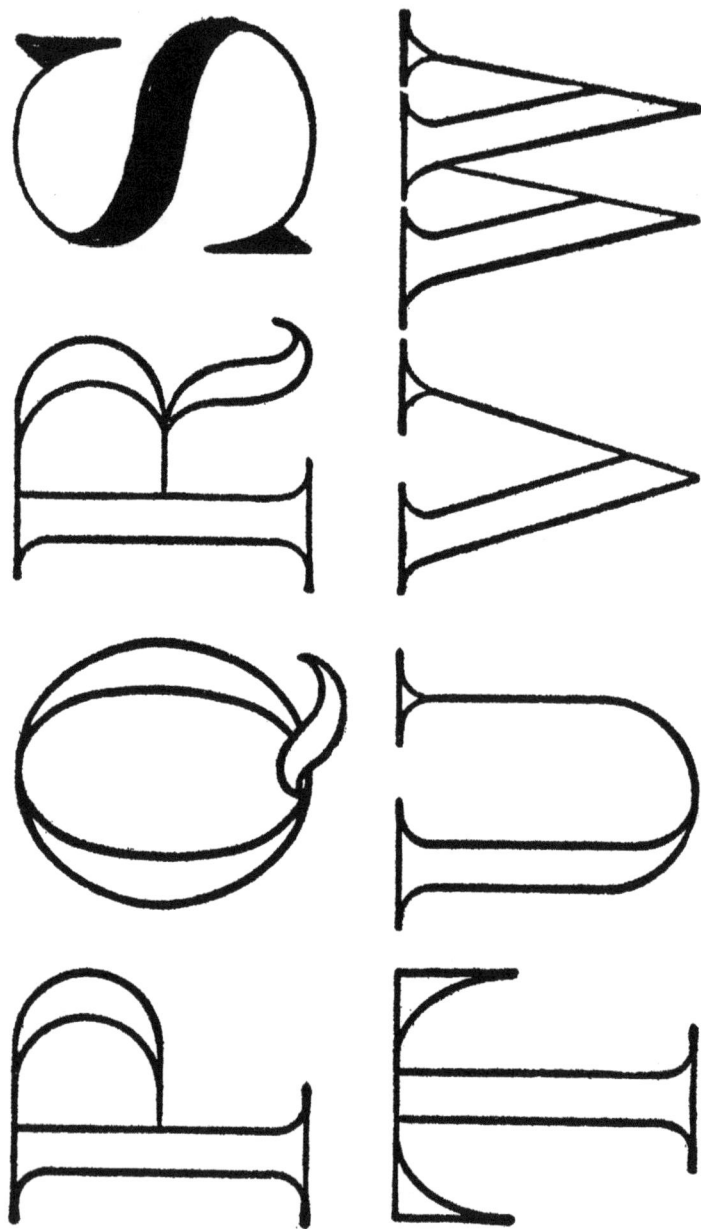

Fig. 105.—Roman Capitals, Open.

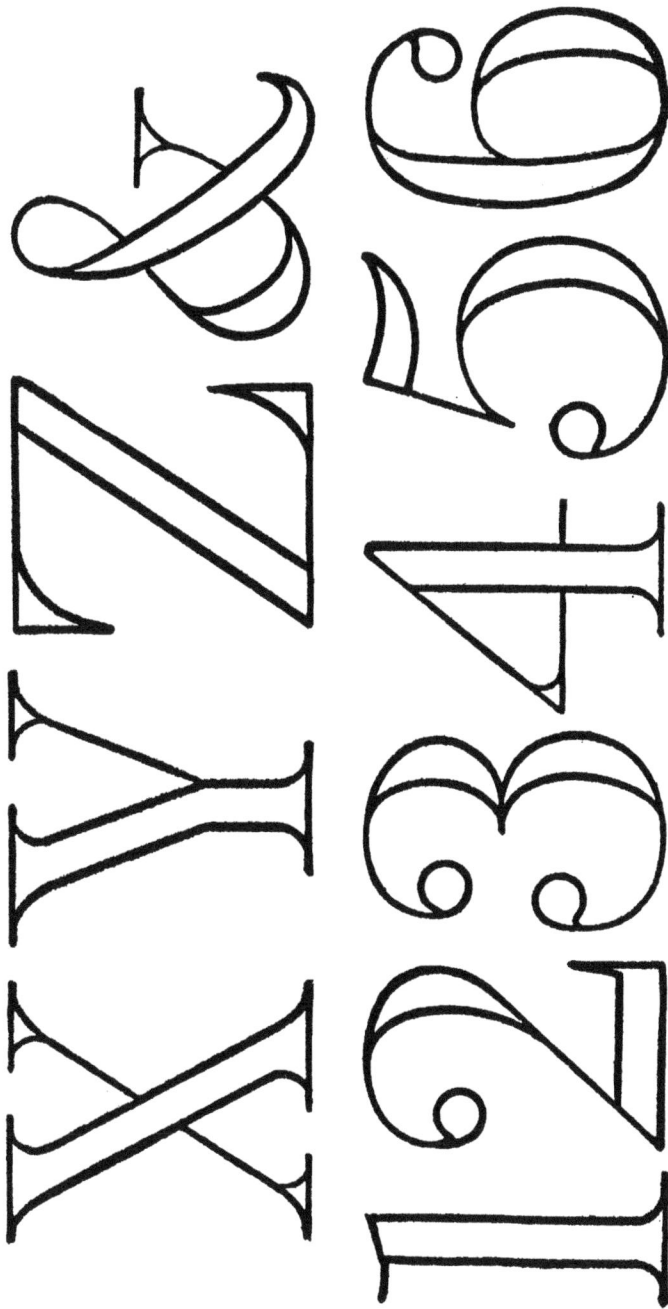

Fig. 106.—Roman Capitals and Numerals, Open.

789

0 . 9 9 0

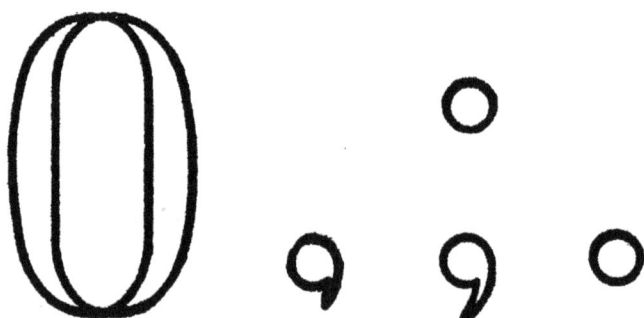

Fig. 107.—Roman Numerals, Stops, and Dashes or Rules.

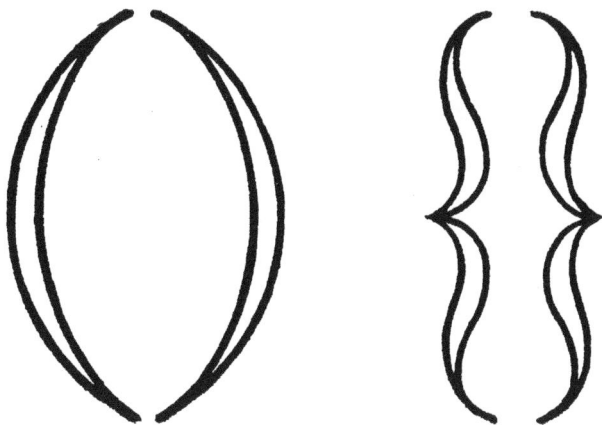

abcdefg

hijklm

nopqrst

uvwxyz

Fig. 108.—Roman Brackets, Braces, and Small Letters.

ABCDE

FGHIJ

KLMN

OPQRS

TUVW

XYZ

Fig. 109.—Egyptian Capitals.

A B C D E

F G H I J

K L M N

O P Q R S

T U V W

X Y Z

Fig. 110.—Italic Capitals.

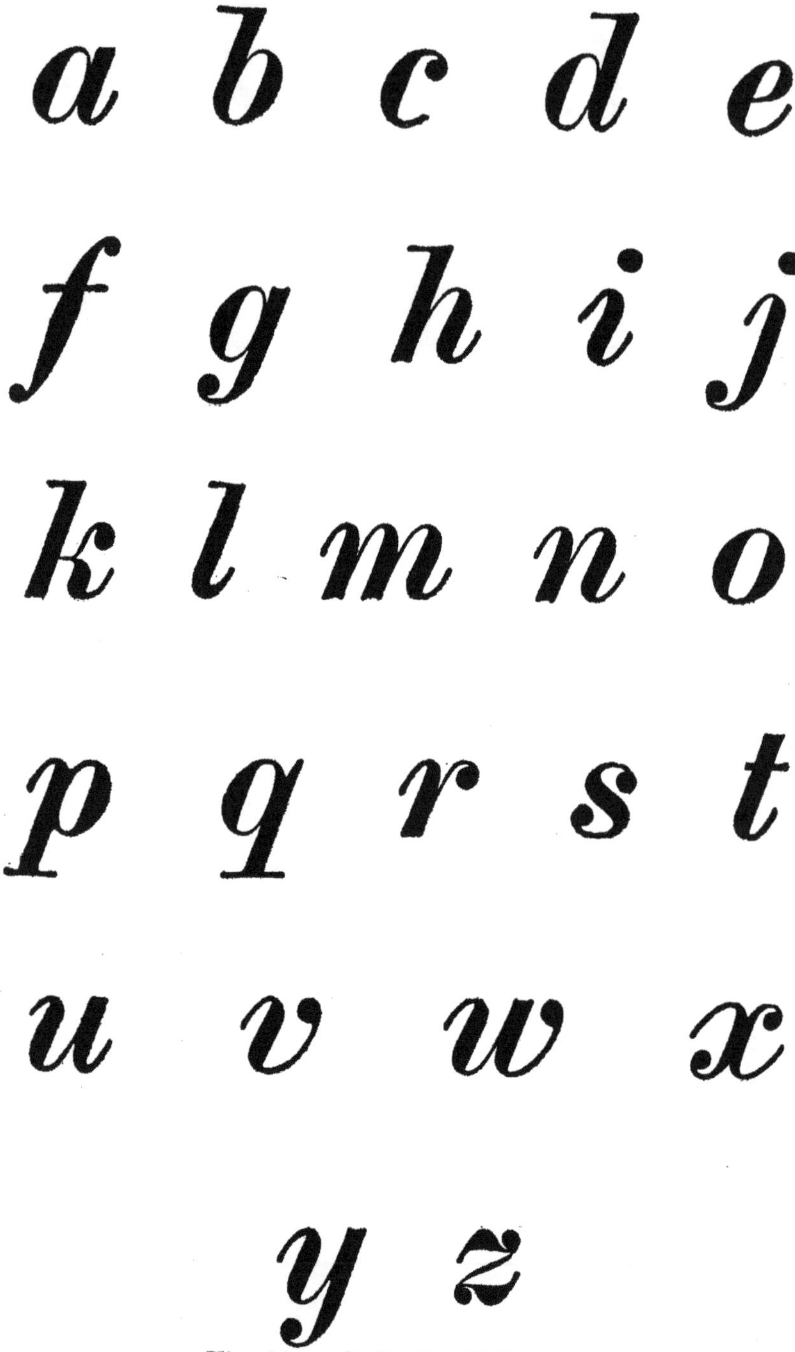

a b c d e

f g h i j

k l m n o

p q r s t

u v w x

y z

Fig. 111.—Italic Small Letters.

A B C D

E F G H

J K L M

N O P Q

R S T U

Fig. 112.—Old English Capitals.

U W X

Y & Z

a b c d e f g

h i j k l m

n o p q r s t

u v w x y z

Fig. 113.—Old English Capitals and Small Letters.

Fig. 114.—Script Capitals.

Fig. 115.—Script Small Letters and Numerals.

ABCDEF
GHIJKL
MNOPQ
RSTUV
WXYZ
& £
123456
7890

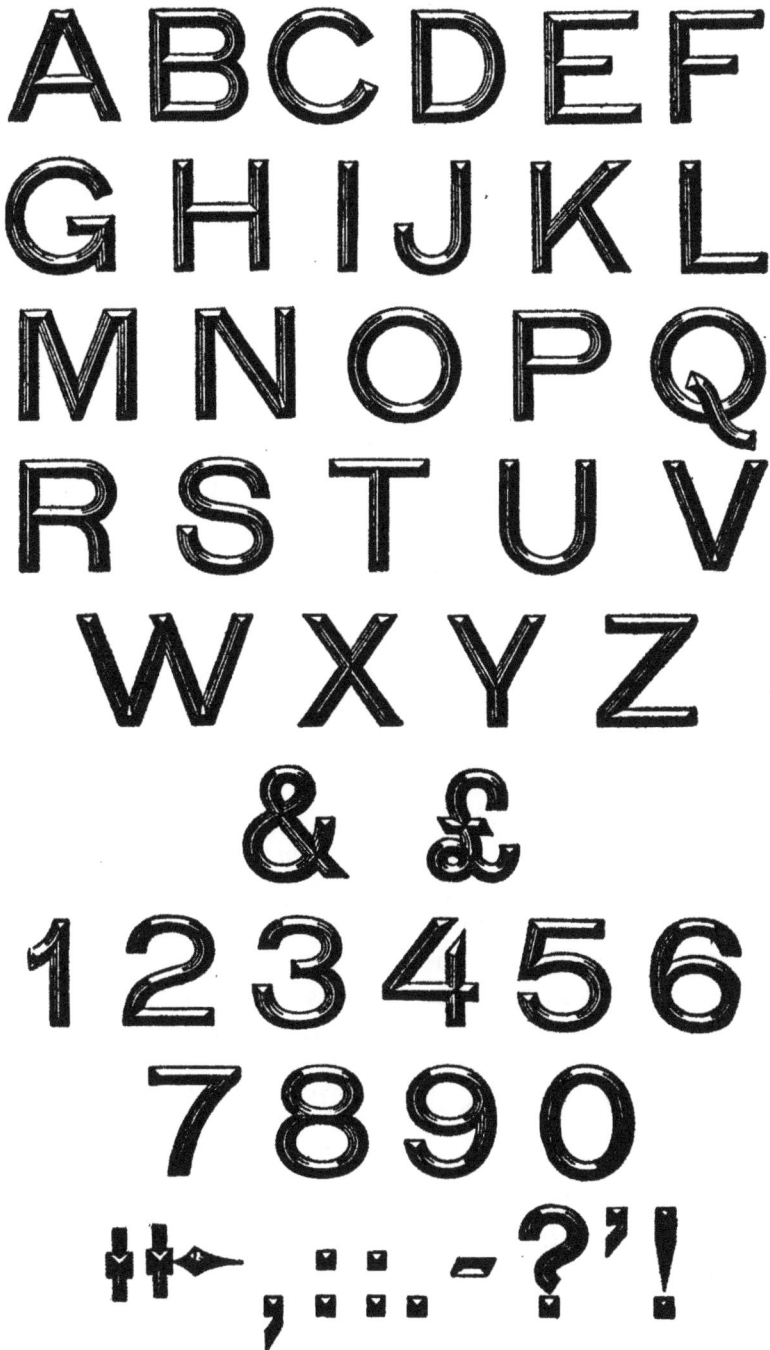

Fig. 116.—Tablet Letters, Numerals, Stops, etc.

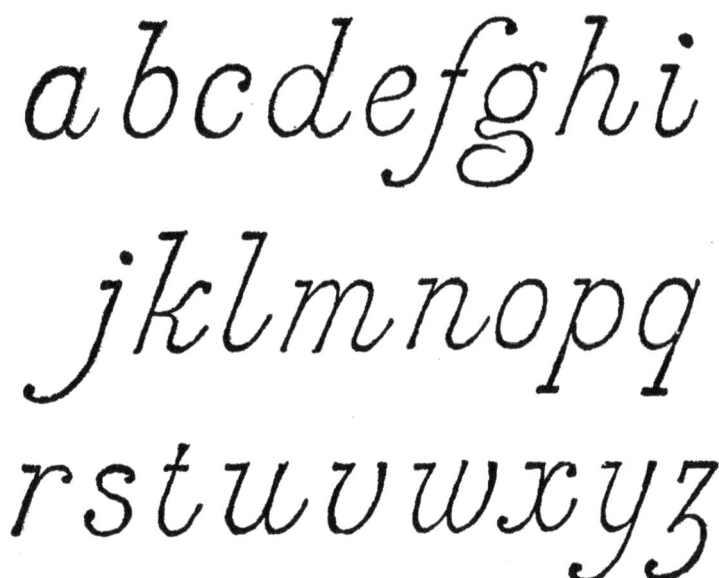

Fig. 117.—Hair-line Italic Small Letters.

When the student has made fair progress in drawing sans-seriff letters, his attention must be directed to more difficult work, such as alphabets of Roman capitals (Figs. 103 to 107). The small letters are shown in Fig. 108, and any special comment seems unnecessary. Excepting the first six letters on p. 74, the capitals are drawn in the style known as "Open Roman." To form them correctly will require more practice than in the case of their predecessors, but as this is one of the most commonly used styles, the letters must not be abandoned till perfection in drawing them has been attained. The relative proportions of each letter as explained in Chapter II. should be carefully observed, and to be in due proportion to the capitals, the small letters should be one half as high.

The student who has practised drawing his letters in outline only—first of all this outline should be drawn very softly with sign-writer's pipe-clay, which costs about 3d. per dozen sticks—may now commence to fill in the alphabet as shown from A to F in Fig 103. He should do this with the camel-hair brush and paint.

having first drawn the outline with the same tool and material the novice will quickly discover that defects show up more plainly when the letters are filled in than when in outline. He will also find that it is possible very often to perfect the shape of letters in the process of filling in, but this should not tempt him to draw a careless outline at the outset.

Having made satisfactory progress with letters, we may next pay attention to the numerals 1 to 0, and the stops, commas, dashes, brackets and braces, as shown in Figs. 106, 107, and 108. The use of these is described in the pages devoted to spacing and display, and it is sufficient for the present to learn how to make them.

The student should soon commence working on the Old English letters, proceeding in the way before recommended, first outlining the letters, and afterwards filling them in. First practise upon the capitals only, Fig. 112, and when fairly successful pay attention to the small letters, Fig. 113. These are the most difficult work yet attempted, but it is easy to practise their formation in leisure moments, and not force the hand nor the patience. These Old English characters must not be neglected altogether, although when once the student can draw with precision he will find it a comparatively easy task to form any ornamental and fancy alphabets and church text letters which he may eventually be called upon to paint.

These lessons on forming alphabets may appropriately conclude with a few remarks on "script," or hand-writing letters, which are illustrated in Figs. 114 and 115. This is the ordinary writing we have all been taught at school, and is known in the copy books as "round-hand." It is much more difficult to execute this writing with the camel-hair pencil than with the pen, but it must be thoroughly practised, as the style is in great demand in sign-writing, and it requires to be done well or should not be attempted.

A sable writer is the best brush for practising "script" writing, and no outline should be made, but a straight line is useful to work upon. The wrist must rest comfortably on the mahl-stick, and the work has to be done in a quick, bold, unhesitating manner. The beginner may advantageously practise writing Old English and "script" letters with pen and ink on good glazed writing paper, and afterwards on an enlarged scale on hot-pressed drawing-paper. If this has been previously done at school and some proficiency has been acquired, such preliminary work is not requisite.

The hardest part of the sign-writer's work is now over. Specimens of the different forms of letters most commonly in use have been given, with instructions for painting them. These are the foundation of other styles and varieties in use at the present day. When once the reader has become complete master of these alphabets, and of the freehand drawing given in the first lessons, he may style himself a sign-writer. He has only to learn what experience will teach him, such as spacing his letters and the proper display of his words.

Some alphabets of modern ornamental and of mediæval style have the face of the letters shaded by sharp clear markings or linings. The thickness or breadth of these lines is symmetrical throughout in some alphabets, in others it is thickest in the middle, and diminishes outwards to the top and bottom of the letter until it becomes a fine hair line. Letters known as Tuscan are of this description, and they have a very gorgeous and rich appearance when well done, especially if the letters are gilded. When being copied for practice, the letters should be enlarged to about three or four inches high, and they will then prove useful for future guidance. The letters should be drawn on separate squares of Bristol board and preserved in a strong envelope or case. They can be made still more useful if coloured in various designs by the method described in the chapter on ticket-writing : thus they will be handy for showing to customers as specimens of style, colour, and workmanship. This suggestion applies equally to all alphabets, and a good way of assuring satisfaction is to

give a customer the opportunity of choosing from specimens before commencing the work, though few sign-
writers consult their customers or study their wishes in
such a way.

Another alphabet is known as Tablet letters; these
represent letters of marble or china affixed to the signboard. Here the shading is all done upon the face of
the letter, and to look well this requires a skilled and
decisive hand, besides a knowledge of the art to get the
proper effect.

Another style of letter is the sunken or incised letter,
which is just the opposite to the Tablet. This is difficult to paint, and the whole effect depends upon clever
shading. The difficulty in shading Tablet and incised
letters is to give each style the appearance of a solid
letter laid on the board or of a sunken letter cut
into it, as the case may be. A complete Tablet alphabet
is given on p. 87, and the letters should be redrawn and
painted on an enlarged scale, so as to learn and judge
the proper effect and the suitability for various purposes.

In these incised letters the depth is the equivalent of
the thickness in raised letters, but there are also the
shadows and reflections, which must be put in carefully
to obtain the desired effect. It is best to let the light
fall on that side visible to the spectator—this will be in
the highest light—and the opposite side in shadow.
The letters are often viewed from below, and also the
light principally strikes down from above, so the
revealed parts at top and bottom should be in shadow.
Prismatic letters are incised, but more elaborate, and
consequently harder to produce successfully.

Letters which form the various styles of plain alphabets comprise the foundation for most of the ornamental alphabets. When the student has fully mastered
the plainer series of letters, he should be ready to
handle with success the more difficult combinations
which a first-class sign-writer is called upon to produce.
It is in such work that the genius of the painter is most

severely tested.   To satisfactorily execute the comparatively simple forms of the Roman, p. 74, sans-seriff,
pp. 67 to 71, and Egyptian alphabets, p. 80, neatness and
finish are the main requirements.   The angles should be
clean and true, the lines straight, and the curves regular.
A considerable amount of dexterity, which can only be
acquired by much practice, is necessary to attain perfection in these particulars.   But when the learner
comes to the more difficult accomplishment of ornamental writing, in addition to this he must familiarise
himself with the general principles of design.   A good
sign-writer will not rèst content with always copying
the productions of others, however much they may be
worthy of imitation.

Writing names on carts and waggons is a very simple
affair, as plain block letters are generally used for all
country rolling stock.   Ordinary paint thinned with a
little turps is generally used for common work of this
kind, and when a lot of it has to be done speed is necessary, so the more simple the diluents the less likely one is
apt to go wrong.   The last coat of paint put on the cart
or waggon is usually mixed with as much boiled oil as
possible, so that it may dry with a good gloss, and also
keep out the weather.   This glossy surface is fatal to
good lettering, as the letters will run ragged at the edges.
Sometimes this may be prevented by using nearly all
turps in the paint used for writing with, or by rubbing
the surface with a little turps, or by wetting with a leather.
If neither of these remedies is effective, repaint the part
where letters are to go.

In what has to follow, there is nothing but
pleasurable and interesting information for the as-
piring sign-writer, and in perusing it he will be adding
to his knowledge without apparent effort.   The expert
sign-writer will always have in the later chapters a
handy book to which he may refer in any case of
uncertainty or doubt.

CHAPTER VI.

SHADED AND FANCY LETTERING.

ORNAMENTAL lettering affords scope for originality, and the scope is practically boundless, there being no limit to the forms which may be given to alphabetical characters. It is necessary, however, to guard against an extravagant use of ornament. As a rule, it should be simple rather than complex, and the style of embellishment should not detract from the legibility of the lettering, for, if this occurs, the result can scarcely be deemed satisfactory ; it must be borne in mind that legibility is the first purpose which the writing has to serve, to which decorative accessories are subordinate.

The style of the lettering must in all cases be in harmony. A common fault, and one very offensive to the educated eye, is the association of styles of lettering and of ornamentation which war with each other in the properties of both time and form.

When proficiency has been attained in the plain styles of lettering, the pupil will find it not difficult to introduce fresh and graceful lines into the plain letters, to ornament their faces and beautify them. He may get many suggestions in this way from ornamental founts, impressions of which appear in typefounders' specimen-books, and from these the sign-writer may work out and adapt ornamental alphabets as required. The specimen-books mentioned contain only a few letters, generally a complete word is printed. Those who need every letter of the alphabet should procure books sold for the special purpose. The following books of alphabets by Delamotte, published by Crosby Lockwood & Son, are useful, and ought to be studied by every sign-writer :—" Mediæval Alphabets and Initials," 4s. ; " Examples of Modern Alphabets,"

2s. 6d. ; and "Ornamental Alphabets," 2s. 6d.   There are several books of a similar kind, published from 1s. upwards, and specimens of various ornamental letters will be found in this handbook.

A "blocked" or "raised" letter is one which stands out in relief, such as solid wood letters, and it is the aim of the sign-writer to imitate this on a flat surface by skilful perspective and colouring.   A "double blocked" letter is one which is blocked out on both sides, or internally and externally.   The "thickness" is the sides or edges, and the ends of a blocked letter ; but only one side and one end are visible to the eye at one time. Letters are generally viewed from below, and commonly shaded on the right, so the bottom and right sides are usually those where the thickness is given   Though this thickness can be put at either side of the letter, or at the top or bottom, it cannot properly be put on both sides at once, because it would be impossible to see both the edges of a solid letter at one and the same time. The same applies to the top and bottom edges.   The "cast" shadow is that which is thrown on to the background by a raised letter through the rays of light shining upon it in an oblique direction : this shadow is on the side opposite to that upon which the rays of light fall.   A graduated thickness is one of graduated tints, in order to represent more vividly the degrees of light that fall on different portions of the thickness ; these may be divided into the high light, the middle or secondary light, and deep shadow.   A graduated thickness is often painted for mere ornamental effect and showy colouring.   The "face" of a letter is its front, which is painted to appear in the highest light, sunken letters excepted.   The explanation of these terms will be better understood on referring to Fig. 118, where A is the face of the letter, B B the thickness or blocking, and C C the shadow, or shade.

Writing in blocked letters is of comparatively recent introduction ; about the year 1840 it first came into vogue, and soon became immensely popular.   It was considered to be a vast improvement on the old style flat lettering, which is now seen only on the commonest work. The real purpose of these blocked letters is to convey to the eye of the spectator, it may be said, an idea of the raised letters cut out in solid wood which no doubt at that date came into sudden and unexpected competition with painted signs. A technical writer of the period remarks : "The projecting letters, formed of

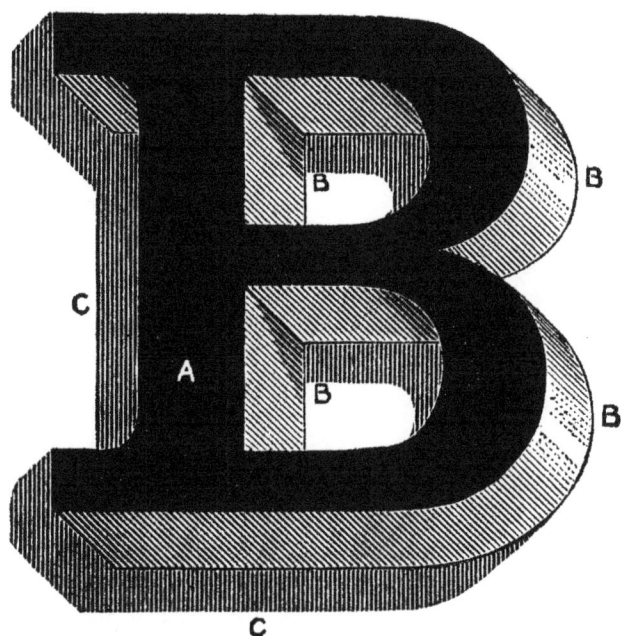

Fig. 118.—Formation of a Blocked or Raised Letter.

wood or metal, have of late become so fashionable that the writers on shop fronts and signboards have had recourse to imitating them, and have produced letters in such bold relief, that they look more real and much better than their wooden rivals."

In blocking-up, each letter must have its thickness outline in its own perspective, which must be the same in each letter, 45° being the angle usually adopted. For plain work, the thickness is usually a darker colour than either the ground on the face of the letter, but there are exceptions even in the simple form of blocked letter. When dealing with light and shade, the side of the letter upon which the light is to strike must be decided upon. When the thickness is shown away from the source of light, its shade colour will be darker than the face of the letter and the ground colour; when it fronts the light, it will be lighter than the ground

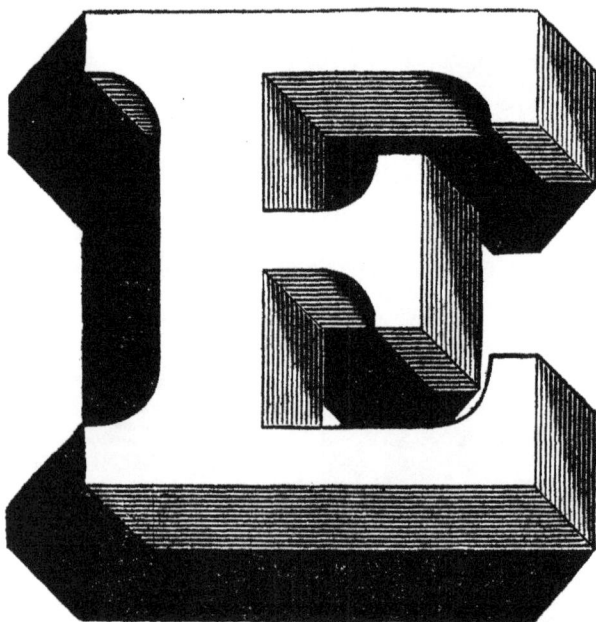

Fig. 119.—Letter with thickness underneath and towards light, shadow on opposite side.

colour, but darker or of a more retiring colour than the face colour of the letter (*see* Figs. 118 to 121.)

It must be remembered that writing on a shop front or on a signboard is generally looked at from below, so that it is a general rule to show thickness at the bottom end of the letters and not at the top (Fig. 119.) A letter to appear as shown in Fig. 120, must be seen from above, but this shading is often done when the letter stands above the point of sight, and it is out of all true perspective. There is much latitude allowed in signwriting, and this anomaly is permitted, as it obtains a

somewhat picturesque effect. In this system the whole
of the painting is between the two horizontal lines
which contain the body of the letters, and though there
is not a single slanting line in any letter, they have
the appearance of projecting, as will be seen on looking
at Fig. 121.

In a graduated thickness, the various tints or
colours must be carefully blended into each other. In
examining the best specimens of sign-writing which

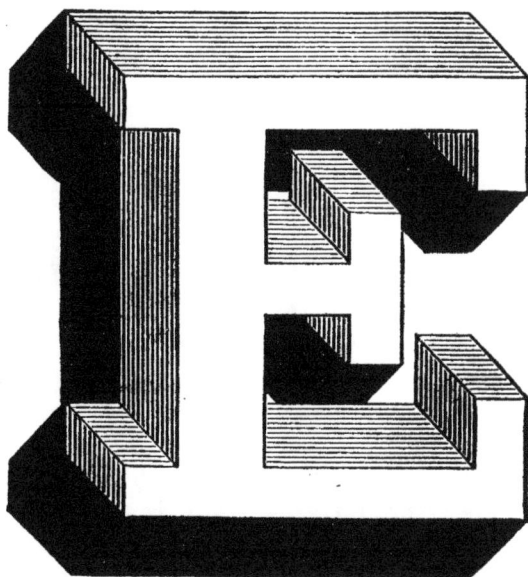

Fig. 120.—Letter with thickness above partly towards light
and partly against, shadow on opposite side.

may be seen in the principal streets of some large
town, one cannot help being struck with the taste and
talent displayed in beautifully blending and colouring
thicknesses, which play an important part in adding an
air of positive grandeur to the work.

To ensure success in the imitation of a raised letter
upon a flat surface it is necessary to be correct in
drawing, colouring, and shading; the drawing must be
true, the colouring bold and effective without being
gaudy, and the shading and gradation appropriate, to

give the subject an appearance of solidity which it has
not in reality. The most beautiful softened thicknesses
are obtained with slow-drying colours, and the judicious
use of the blender. Thicknesses may be bright or
otherwise, according to the scheme of colouring employed by the operator.

However bright in colour the body and thickness
may be, when a cast shadow is added it must be quiet in
tone, being a mere glaze on the ground to make it darker
where the shadow falls. The siennas, umbers, Vandyke
brown, and asphaltum are good glazing colours for
rendering cast shadows. Letters may be shadowed

Fig. 121.—Letters with thickness against light and without
slanting lines.

either on the same side as the thickness or on the
opposite side; the latter system is generally adopted,
and in this the thickness receives the rays of light, and
is therefore painted in a brighter colour than if it were
represented as in the shade. It is satisfactory if painted
the same colour as the face of the letter, but in a somewhat darker shade. When a thickness faces the light
it is frequently put in with two or three gradations of
tint, the lightest where the edge of the letter catches
most light, and the darkest in the under portions of the
arms and bottom end of the letter. It always gives
better effect to the whole when the bottom of the letter
is painted a darker shade, as this portion of a projecting
letter must necessarily be in the deepest shadow. The
bottom portion of all letters throws a cast shadow, and
these follow beneath the thickness, so the shadow

always falls upon portions of such thickness, whichever side it is on. When a letter has its cast shadow and its thickness on the same side, and away from the source of light, the thickness is naturally darker than the face of the letter, and the shadow is preferably of a shade not far removed from black.

The source of light is the pivot upon which turns the colouring and shading of a letter. When writing signs for exposure to the open daylight, where the sun, that lights all things, is constantly on the move, it would be impossible to so arrange shadows that they shall always appear in a direction opposite to that from which the sun is shining, because if correct in the morning, it would not be so in the afternoon. The best arrangement is to consult the position in which the sign is situated, notice from which direction the light is strongest during the greater part of the day, and adapt the light and shade of the work so as to conform with nature, as far as it can, in a pleasing and truthful manner.

Many specimens of sign-writing have been treated in a purely conventional manner : for instance, letters without blocking or thickness possessing a cast shadow. Considering that the letters appear to lie quite flat upon the surface, the question arises, what is there to throw this shadow. Here the sign-writer disregards the laws of shading when painting blockless letters with a cast shadow.

In treating blocked or raised letters on perspective lines, the angle of perspective used for different sets of alphabets may to a great extent be left to the writer's discretion, but all letters on the same line must have the same angle or inclination. The ordinary set-square, with an angle of 45° is found to be most useful for setting out the proper inclination of the thicknesses. This plan is recommended as the best way to educate both the eye and the hand. A variety of alphabets are given on pp. 80 to 82, and the two complete perspective alphabets (Figs. 122 and 123), on pp. 100 and 101, will prove of value in actual practice.

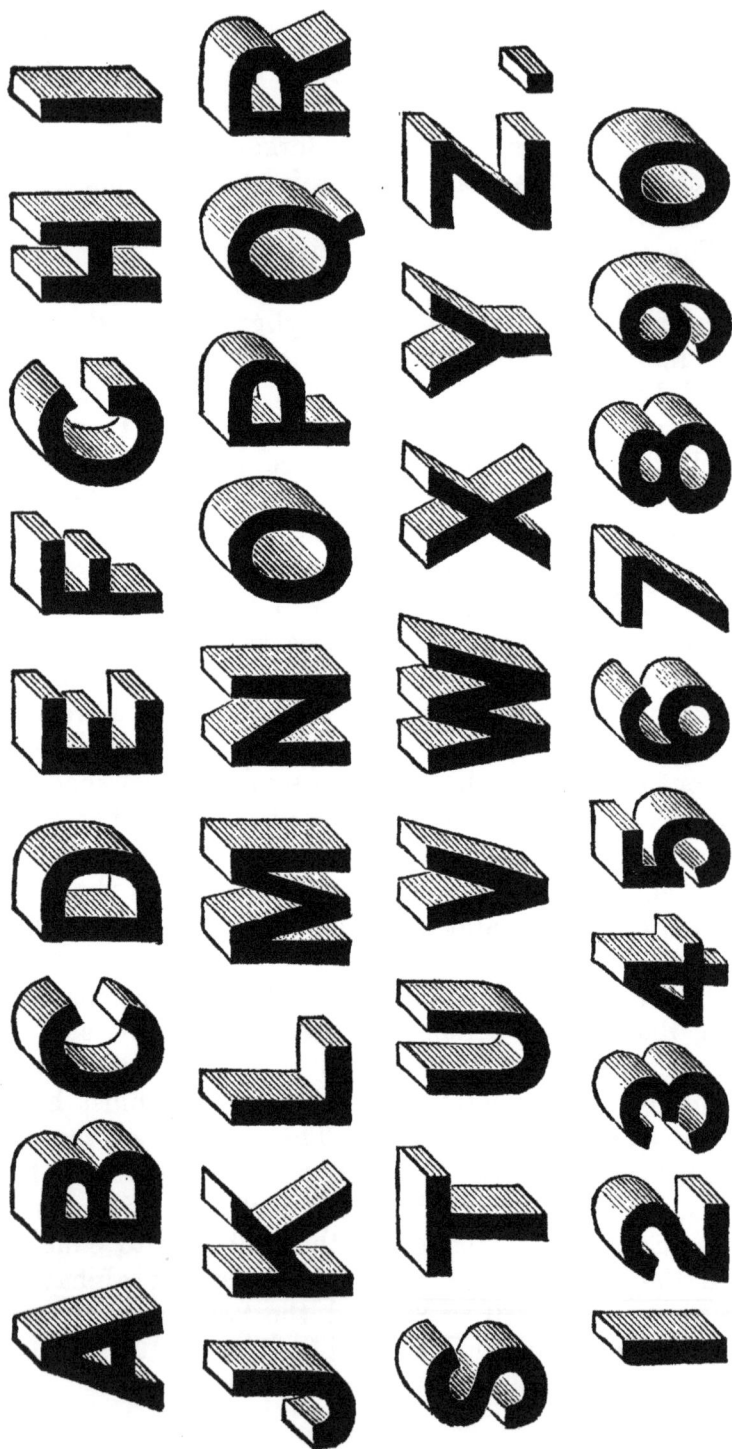

Fig. 122.—Sans-serif Alphabet and Numerals in Perspective.

Fig. 123.—Italian Alphabet in Perspective.

Church text requires separate treatment. A vast amount of this work is done within churches, and such work is probably highly remunerative. Much of it borders on the art of illuminating, but an efficient sign-writer takes up certain branches of this work. Previous training should eminently fit him for executing such work with little extra study and preparation, and self-help and self-tuition may be relied upon as far as needed. The sign-writer who attains proficiency in this

Fig. 124.—Ornamental Lettering for Church Work—
Initial Letter.

branch of decorative art, will find it to be the means of increasing his income, and for this reason he should give illuminating consideration.

For church inscriptions the use of illuminated capitals, like Fig. 124, and mediæval lettering, like the alphabet, Figs. 125, 126, are now much in vogue. Ordinarily, Scripture texts should be painted on the plain walls in two colours only, the capitals being red, red and black, or blue, and the small letters red, blue or black. The colour may be in such tints as stand out best against the ground colour on the wall. When painted, a wall is generally stone colour, so the plain colours look the best. Walls are sometimes painted in the many-coloured style of decoration. Here the lettering is more showy in colour, to be in keeping with the rest of the decoration. In mediæval alphabets, it is necessary to use the various old-style space ornaments and accessories (Figs. 127, 128), such as quatrefoils, dots singly and in clusters, stars, etc.

In church texts the words are frequently divided by these ornaments or stops. This method was adopted by the olden time illuminators, and it is still followed by modern members of the craft. In this class of lettering care has to be taken to use only the letters of one alphabet, and not to mix with them some other letter, which is apt to occur where the student has been exercising with a great many alphabets of different dates and countries. To avoid this, always carry specimen books for reference.

Alphabets antecedent to the twelfth century are not intelligible to the majority of modern readers. The sign-writer may have in his book Celtic and Anglo-Saxon characters as curiosities, but not for everyday use. They may be required when lettering some archæological object, but that is all.

In church lettering the point to consider is which alphabets to employ that shall be both readable and appropriate to the scheme of decoration in hand. In these days, when all can read and write, inscriptions should be decipherable by all, and this these obsolete alphabets are certainly not.

Much text lettering is done upon zinc in the shape of scrolls, pulpit panels, etc., so the following recipe is appended.

To prepare zinc for painting upon.—In sixty-four parts of water, dissolve one part of chloride of copper, one of

Fig. 125.—Mediæval Capitals.

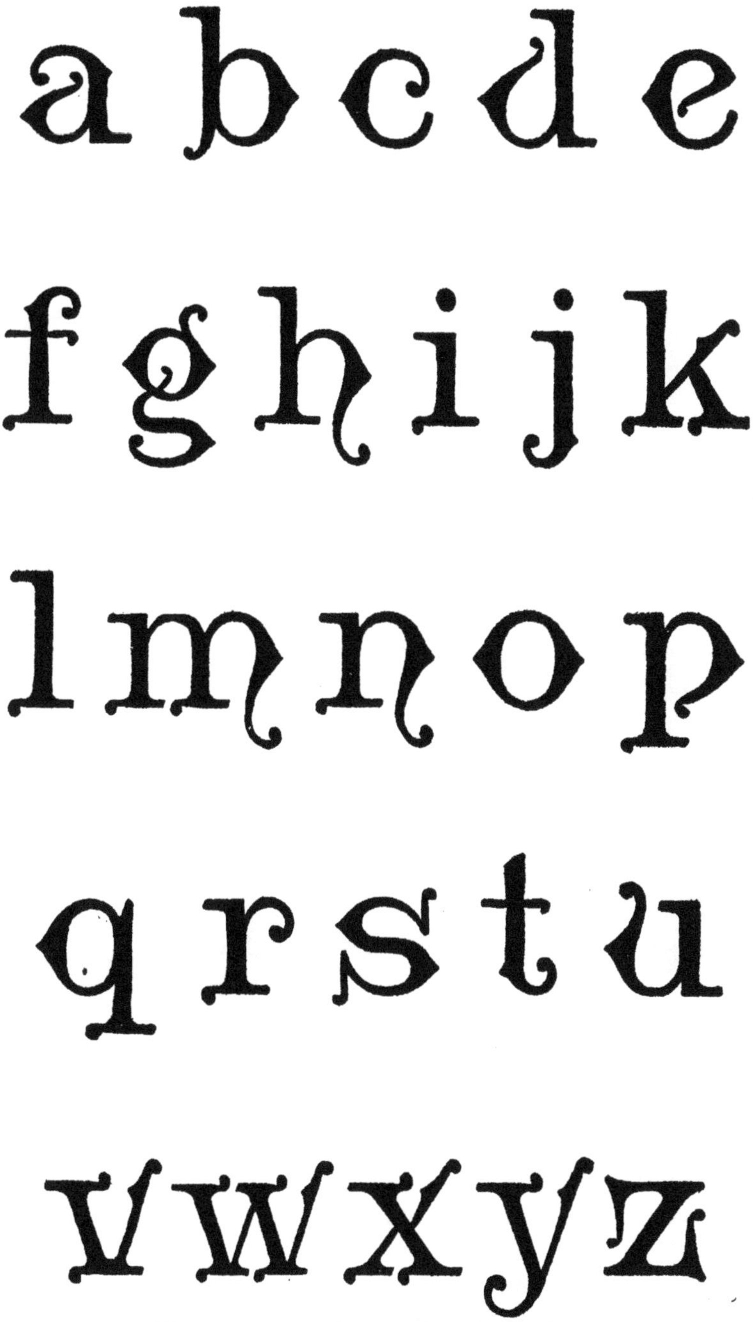

a b c d e

f g h i j k

l m n o p

q r s t u

v w x y z

Fig. 126.—Mediæval Small Letters.

nitrate of copper, and one of sal-ammoniac, and add one
part of commercial hydrochloric acid; brush the zinc
over with this mixture, which gives it a deep black; leave
it to dry for twenty-four hours, when any oil-colour will

Fig. 127.—Ornaments for Church Work—A, Corners;
B, Centre; C, Border; D, Maltese Cross; E, Trefoil;
F. Quatrefoils.

firmly adhere to it and withstand both heat and damp.
To prepare zinc for gold lettering, first brush over all
the surface the following blackening mixture, and allow
it twenty-four hours to dry.   Mix 1 oz. each of copper
chloride, copper nitrate, and sal-ammoniac together;
add the mixture to 3 pints of water, and stir in half a

Fig. 128.—Ornaments for Church Work—H, Circles, K,
Ribbon End; L, Diamond Cluster; M, Cross; N, Star; O,
Tablet End; P, Scroll End.

wineglassful of spirits of salts. This will turn the surface of the zinc a deep black, and the prepared surface will take oil-paint well. Gild with good leaf gold in the usual way, and varnish with good clear varnish. This method will ensure durability to the lettering.

Having digested the subjects of ornamental and church lettering, and other matter appertaining thereto, it remains only to draw attention to other much-used forms of letters. This refers principally to letters that have to be somewhat distorted in shape to suit the exigences of space, which in some cases is excessive, and in others inadequate. First take the case of having to write a short name on a long narrow surface. The ordinary-shaped letter would not fit or look well in such a case, we therefore expand it, so that it may fill the long space better, and yet be sufficiently low in height to come within the width of the surface and allow for shading, etc.

When it is desired to fill an extra long line with expanded letters, the expansion must be proportionate throughout, so that the work may have a symmetrical appearance. A letter low enough for the purpose is selected, and this is expanded widthways to an extent which would be proper to a higher letter.

This expansion will be made with mathematical precision by the following method :—Suppose the letters W O R K are to be painted on a signboard 4 ft. long by 1 ft. 6 in. wide, and that these letters, in their usual form and properly spaced, extend to 2 ft., it will therefore be necessary to expand them to about 3 ft. Now refer to the diagram, Fig. 129, which is drawn approximately to scale. The normal letters extend, from A to B., 2 ft., and without increasing their height we have to spread them out 1 ft., so that they will extend from C to D. At any convenient distance below, having the normal letters as shown at A B, rule two parallel lines 1 ft. apart, and 3 ft. long from C to D, and draw a line from A to

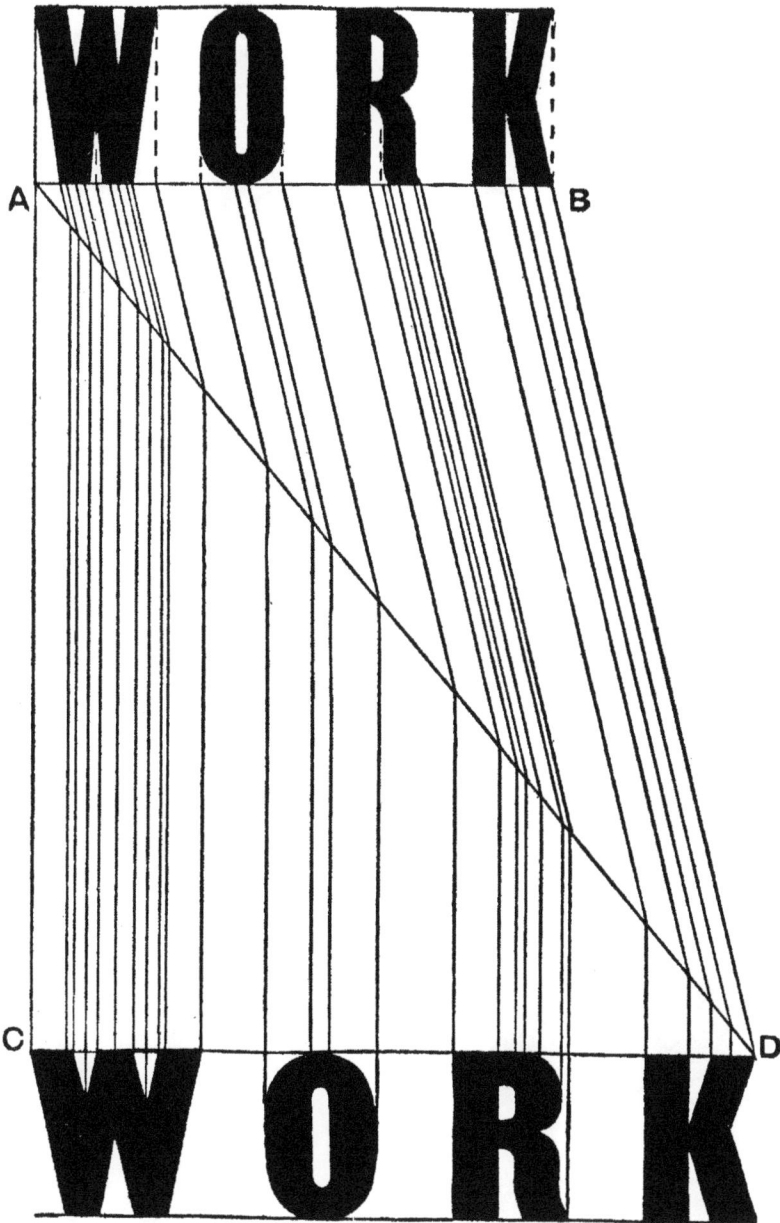

Fig. 129.—Method of Expanding or Condensing Letters.

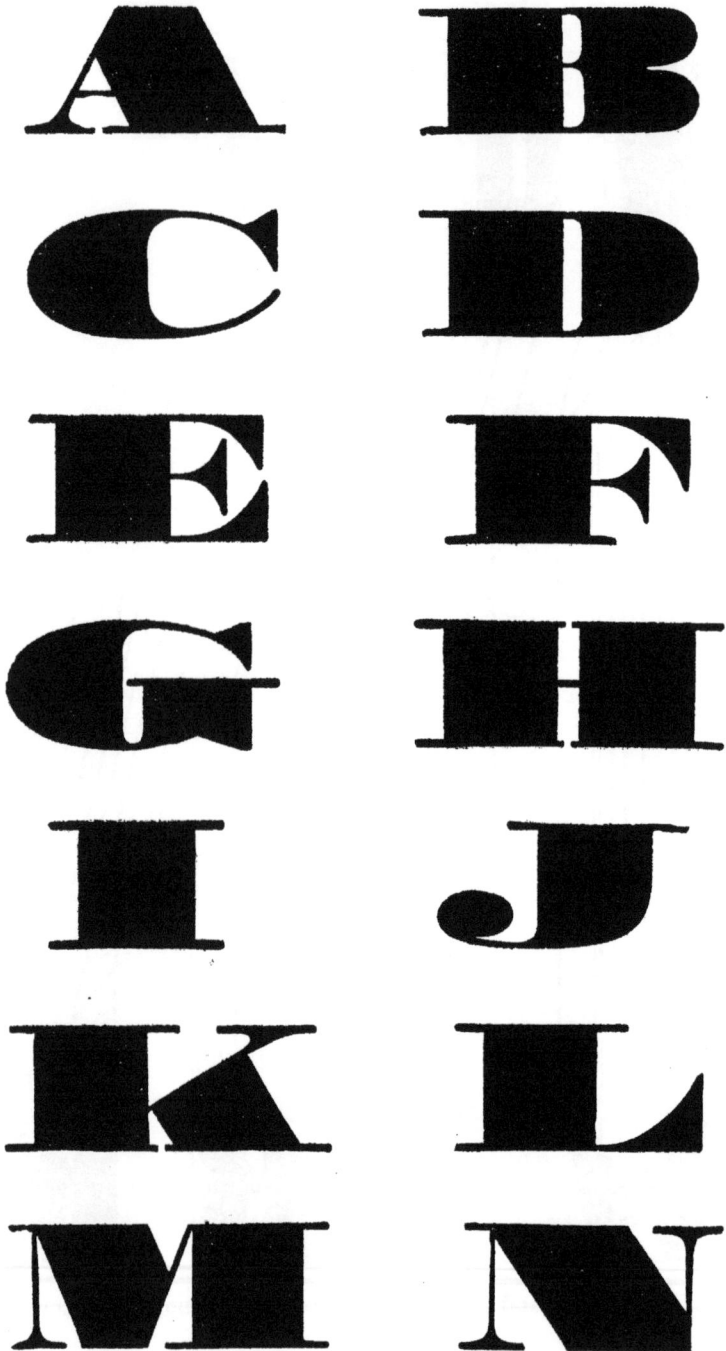

Fig. 130.—Expanded Letters.

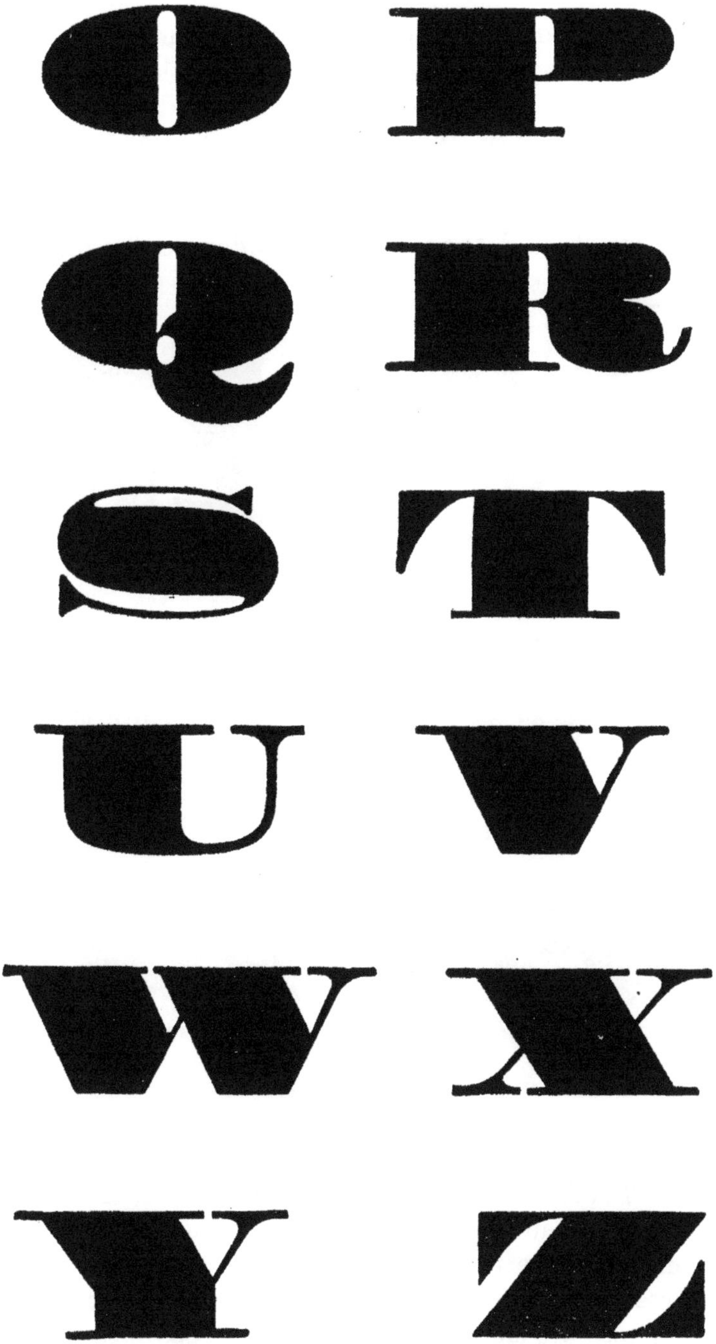

O P
Q R
S T
U V
W X
Y Z

Fig. 131.—Expanded Letters.

D.   Parallel to the line B D draw lines from the
bottoms of the row of letters on A B to the line A D ;
from the points where these lines cut A D draw vertical
lines to the line C D.   From these lines proceed to draw
in the bottom letters ; the result will be as shown in
Fig. 129.   By this method letters can be extended to any
desired width, and they may be condensed by making

Fig. 132.—Elongated
or Condensed Letters.

Fig. 133.—Compressed Letters.

the line C D shorter than the line A B.   In practice,
the student may either work out the problem as in a
scale drawing, or he may draw the letters full size on
two lengths of lining paper tacked to a wall or floor.
The outline of the extended letters would then be prepared for pouncing the design upon the signboard.

Fig. 134.—Expanded Ionic Letters.

Elongated or condensed letters are the reverse of the
last-named series, and are used principally where the
surface to be lettered is short in length, but of unusual
height.   These elongated or condensed letters, shown in
Fig. 132, come in useful on certain occasions, as do also
the compressed letters, shown in Fig. 133.

Three special kinds of fancy letters require consideration.   These are slanting letters, thicknessed letters, and
shaded letters.   When the limbs corresponding to the

uprights in a plain block alphabet are made to lean to one side, it is necessary to draw the guide-lines at that angle. This is done by laying the straight-edge and set-square upon the slate sufficiently askew to obtain the required result.

For writing a letter to appear as if it had thickness as well as length and breadth, it is as well to consider what lines would actually appear to the eye of a person looking at such a solid letter from the side and point of view to be represented : this consideration once fixed in the mind will make the counterfeit presentment easy. In a solid letter there are two sets of edges : one set in contact with the surface to which the letter is fixed, the other set at a regular distance in front of that surface, as far from it as the letter is thick. The whole of the front set of edges will be seen by a person looking at the letter, but only so much of the back set as is not hidden by the front. . Therefore, in writing an imitation solid letter, it is necessary to see that the same appearance is presented to the eye. The rule to follow is to draw the front set of edges and fill the body in first. From the corners of these a number of parallel lines are drawn, their length being according to the thickness to be represented. These lines are drawn from each angle of the letter, where, by doing so, they do not cross the face of the letter. . In the case of curved letters it is necessary to draw, from each centre round which the curves are struck, a line parallel to and of the same length as those drawn from the corners. The ends of these lines from centres are then used as fresh centres from which to draw a duplicate series of curves, which will thus be parallel to the originals. The thicknessing outline, in short, is an exact repetition of the original outline, drawn a little to the right or left of it, and a little above or below it ; the space between the two outlines, as far as it is not covered by the bodying-in of the original letter, is filled in with a tint between that of the front of the letter and that of the background.

Shading, properly done, entails a rather close adherence to the rules governing the art of delineating shadows, this art being known by the pleasant name of sciagraphy. What is most often called or taken for shading is merely the outlining of a wide thicknessing and its subsequent division into two parts, that farthest from the original being coloured black or some sombre tint, and that next to the letter as in the case of ordinary thicknessing. The actual shape of the shadow cast by a solid letter upon a flat ground resembles the letter only in part, and unless drawn correctly, will look very bad. Besides the lines bounding the face of the letter, shadows are cast by those others which stand out at the angles, upright from the background, and form the edges of the thickness ; and when curved edges come to be dealt with, a correct representation by mechanical means really requires the application of the elaborate work used in mechanical perspective. This part of the art, then, can be safely neglected for the present. When thicknessed letters are drawn, it is necessary to allow an extra space between each letter, and to have the limb-thickness more slender than it would be if it had not to be thicknessed.

Specimen alphabets, selected from good examples, will be of infinite use to the novice in writing signs, tickets, and posters.

CHAPTER VII.

PAINTING A SIGNBOARD.

HAVING discussed various styles of letters and the method of forming them with true and graceful outline, we will now proceed to put them to practical use in setting out and lettering a sign. Taking the signboard as properly prepared and quite ready to work upon, start by damping the whole surface with a wet chamois leather. This simple process must always be gone through, otherwise trouble will arise from the colours running on the ground colour and leaving a ragged edge instead of a sharp clear outline. This can be rectified only by repeatedly going over the same outline, with the effect of deteriorating the quality of the completed work, and even this will not always remedy the evil. If, after damping the board, the colours run, another rub should be given with the leather, and should that fail it may be concluded that there is too much oil in the colour, and also it may be too thick ; in this case the addition of a little turpentine will at once prevent the colour from running, and also make it flow easier from the brush.

The size and character of the letters being determined upon, strike the necessary lines to contain them, and proceed to set out the writing with prepared pipeclay, as mentioned in chapter V.

Much depends upon this setting-out and spacing of the letters. It may mar or make the success ; for if badly set out the whole work will look clumsy and inartistic, no matter how well shaped the letters may be. First mark out the whole of the letters in a light and sketchy manner, taking pains to make them fill up the board evenly. If when finished they do not all come in properly, wipe out the chalk marks with the damp leather and try again. Care must be taken not to press the pipeclay upon the surface of the signboard, as it will leave marks that cannot be removed. Practice will soon enable the young writer to set out letters with exactness, but the spacing of the letters themselves, that is, their distance one from another, has also to be considered. In sign-writing, the letters A, C, G, J, K, O, Q, P, V, W and Y require to be placed closer to their neighbours on either side than do the rest of the letters, for the reason that they are not of the same width throughout, and therefore leave more space between them and the next letter. Reference to any large printed letters or to the specimen words given on p. 73, which are evenly spaced, will show this apparently unequal spacing. The novice at sign-writing should endeavour to avoid the appearance of uneven spacing, which evenly spaced letters always give. Close spacing should be the rule with all elongated letters (*see* Fig. 132). These would have a most undesirable effect if widely spaced ; but with expanded letters wide spacing is very suitable.

Whatever the matter may be it must be exactly in the centre of the board, with an equal space or margin at each end. Want of skill in a writer is clearly displayed in the careless arrangement of a name or other word in large letters, which leaves a margin wider at one end of the board than at the other, yet through indifferent spacing this fault is frequently seen.

For the spacing of large letters on high walls no fixed rule can be followed, as the letters must be formed as to size and spacing to suit the circumstances of the case, and it is seldom that these are precisely alike. An experienced writer finds no trouble in doing this, but a novice will find it easier to first measure the space on the wall that has to be lettered and then to arrange the matter on a similar space near the ground. When the size and spacing of all the letters are satisfactory, full measurements may be taken and these jotted down in a book ; then, by the aid of these and a measuring rod, he can proceed to set out the work on the end of a

house or in any other high situation. All this is really
not difficult, and opportunity should, if possible, be found
to watch a good sign-writer at work, as this will teach
more than pages of instructions.

Supposing the letters to be properly spaced and
marked out, we next prepare to outline them in colour.
The pencil is got into working order by dipping it in a
little "turps" and wiping out any excess with a piece of
rag. Sufficient colour is spread upon the palette with the
palette knife, and it is thinned out to a proper working
consistency. No precise information can be given as to
the best working consistency of a paint, but it should be
somewhat thicker than rich cream. When too thick it
will not flow freely from the brush, when too thin, it will
not cover sufficiently, and will also very likely run. A little
variation either way from the correct consistency may put
everything out of order, and the workman out of temper.

The letters should be outlined boldly with a pencil
well charged with colour, which should not leave the
surface till the outline is complete from top to bottom.
Many beginners make their outlines in a series of short
strokes, and occasionally stop in the middle of a line to
recharge the pencil with colour. This makes shaky outlines, and betrays the nervous, unpractised hand. It
may happen that the pencil will not hold sufficient
colour to enable the operator to work from top to bottom
without a break in very large letters ; but, as such letters
are generally at a good height, distance softens imperfect
or ragged outlines. Before starting on every fresh line
the pencil should be refilled with paint, and it will generally hold out to the end. Remember that the larger the
letter the larger the brush and the greater its holding
capacities, so there need be no excuse for short, uneven
strokes in any work of moderate size.

It is more difficult for an unpractised hand to make
a long line in one continuous stroke than in two or
three, but the beginner must not give way to the latter
faulty and unworkmanlike method, or he will have
greater difficulty in shaking himself free from it

afterwards. The hand may not rest on the sign ; if it be unsteady the wrist should rest on the mahl-stick, or on the wrist of the left hand ; never allow the right hand to support itself on the sign, or it will be cramped and hindered in its free movement. In curved letters this is especially so, as a bold, free, and pliable hand is necessary for their correct formation. It is good practice for the student to make all his outlines of a uniform thickness throughout ; this he will find somewhat hard to accomplish at the outset.

When the outlining is complete, the letters are filled in with a short thick brush, of the pattern shown at Figs. 65 and 66), then the whole is left to dry. On the succeeding day, any thicknesses are added and the shadows are put in, and any little defects are touched up. We may then consider our sign finished and ready for varnishing. If the work is surrounded with border, corners, or other ornaments, they are painted at the same time as the letters, and the whole completed together. Always use the point of the pencil in outlining, to get a straight, even line ; when used on its side, the pencil bulges or shrinks under the varying pressure of the hand, and a waved line is the result.

Italic and script lettering must be kept all to the same slope or slant, and the sign-writer had better make himself a few set squares, which may be used as guides for this purpose. Italic letters should not slant so much as ordinary script or writing characters, hence at least two set squares would be necessary. In script writing the capitals should be just double the height of the small letters. Script writing is often used for milliners' and such-like businesses, for which purpose it seems very appropriate, especially when gold letters are used on a black ground. The sign-writer should always endeavour to adopt the style of letter appropriate to the trade to which the sign refers as far as this is practicable. Some businesses allow of much more gaudy colouring than others, as already pointed out in a previous chapter.

When varnishing the completed work, it is better to

give three thin coats, well worked, than two thick ones. Each coat of varnish must be allowed to dry thoroughly hard before applying the next. This will do much towards preventing the sun from cracking the varnish and blistering the paint.

Although it may be that the laws of perspective are not always faithfully followed by the sign-writer, he should, nevertheless, completely master the whole science of perspective, so that he can readily adapt it to his everyday requirements.

The general principles of perspective are fully explained in treatises devoted to the subject. Here we must be content to point out a few examples of sign-writers' perspective. Readers who care to study the subject fully will find it dealt with in "The Principles of Perspective," by Trobridge, published by Cassell & Co., at 1s. 6d. Those who followed the advice given in an earlier chapter of this hand-book, and have a black board, will have the means to work out the problems and to practise the various letters with the greatest facility.

Most sign-writers have sufficient knowledge of perspective to enable them to carry out designs with a passable semblance of truth. Occasionally, however, a glaring slip is made, through want of knowledge of the proper application of perspective lines. The best sign-writers, in order to give themselves freedom of action and plenty of scope in carrying out their designs, use but few lines. The beginner should follow the same course, otherwise he will be hampered in his movements, and an awkward, stilted job may be the result. Linear and aërial perspective may both be applied to sign-writing, and plenty of practice on the blackboard will make the student proficient and expert, so that he can dispense with complicated lines to guide him in putting letters in perspective, the educated eye alone being sufficient. A difficult arrangement should always be drawn on paper, and to scale, in true perspective. Such work is best done at home, where the requisite

Fig. 135.—Simple Method of Drawing Letters in Perspective.

Fig. 136.—Example of Treatment in Perspective.

tools are at hand, including mathematical instruments, squares, and drawing-board. The workman may then transfer this design to the signboard, enlarging it and adapting the perspective as height and position may require.

In sign-writing, as in picture-drawing, there is but one point of sight and one horizontal line for each row of letters. The spectator can only see from one point at one and the same time. He cannot see the first row of letters from one point and at the same time see the second row from another point. Lettering of this description has all top and bottom lines inclined to one vanishing point, which is situated on the horizontal line. This may be explained by the aid of a diagram (Fig. 135).

To set out a perspective drawing take an oblong piece of paper, and draw the horizontal line across the centre, from A to A. Then decide upon the vanishing point, which in this case is at B. In the case of raised or shaded letters, as the lines of the thicknesses run in an opposite direction, there must be another vanishing point on the left at C. This second point has nothing to do with the body part of the letters, and it is only called into use for shading. Next decide upon the height of the first letter on the left; draw this in, and strike two lines, D, D, respectively, from the top and bottom, to the vanishing point, B, and these two lines mark the space within which the letters must be kept. The diagram shows the letters diminished not only in height but also in breadth as they recede towards the vanishing point, B. The outline of the thickness for each letter must retire towards the point C, as shown by the dotted lines.

Fig. 138 is a specimen of sign-writing treated in the way described, but a much more effective way of treating a perspective of this class is by the method shown at Fig. 136. This way of treating a sign makes a most attractive and striking advertisement for some purposes. Fig. 137 shows an instance of the point of

Fig. 137—Perspective Lettering with Point of Sight in Centre.

Fig. 138—Treatment of Advertising Sign in Perspective.

sight in the centre of the board at A, and a vanishing point on either side at B, B. In the name HIGGINS, the second G is the middle letter, and it is drawn exactly in the centre of the board, the size determined upon, and the vanishing lines drawn on each side accordingly.

A short sign, rendered necessary by cramped space, is a good one upon which to apply this method, and it is made more showy and complete by the addition of an oval border. To strike perspective lines, when the vanishing points are situated outside the margin of the signboard, is in many cases impossible. There is, however, a method of transferring perspective lines from a scale drawing on to a larger surface, which is both easy and accurate. This plan is used in scene-painting, and there is no reason why it should not be used in lettering, with slight modification. Standing directly facing the centre of a signboard, having projecting letters tacked on the board, we see only the front surface of the centre letter, and not the sides of it ; of the letters to the right we see the front and left side only of the letter, of the letters to the left the front and right side only of letters. If we stand to the left of the sign, we see all the left-hand edges, and if we go to the right we see the right-hand thicknesses, the point of sight being in the first case to the left and in the second to the right. We cannot conveniently have this point in the centre, but we may have it on the right or the left, and the former is in most general use.

In shading letters the general practice is to have a fresh vanishing point for each, which in effect means that most sign-writers draw all the receding lines of shadows and of thicknesses at an angle of 45°. An expert can do this by the eye alone. The beginner should use a set-square for the purpose, as badly shaded letters spoil a job. An otherwise perfect letter is made to appear out of the perpendicular and has a tumble-down appearance if the shading be bad.

We may now describe the method of painting some of those common ornaments, as some call them, which

the sign-writer is often called upon to paint upon a
tradesman's sign or upon a trade cart. We frequently
see best work surrounded with a plain or an ornamental
border, and this cannot well be dispensed with, even by
the writer who is accustomed only to the simplest of work.

Fig. 139.—Plain Board, with screw-heads at corners.

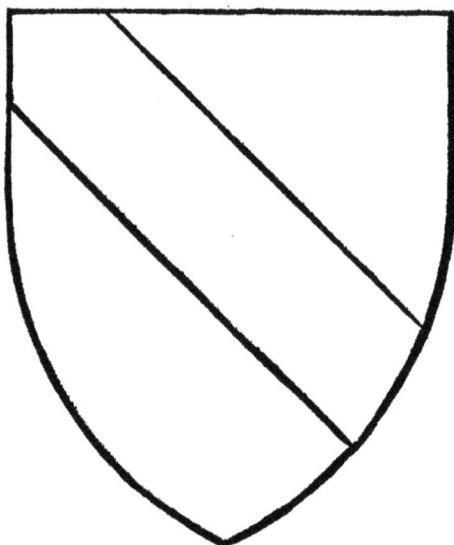

Fig 140.—Plain Shield.

The accompanying outline drawings show some of
the subjects most frequently employed, and it is necessary that the sign-writer should know how to draw these
with accuracy. They are given only as copies for repeated practice. In drawing these examples compasses
and rule are permissible, but they may be drawn freehand for a time.

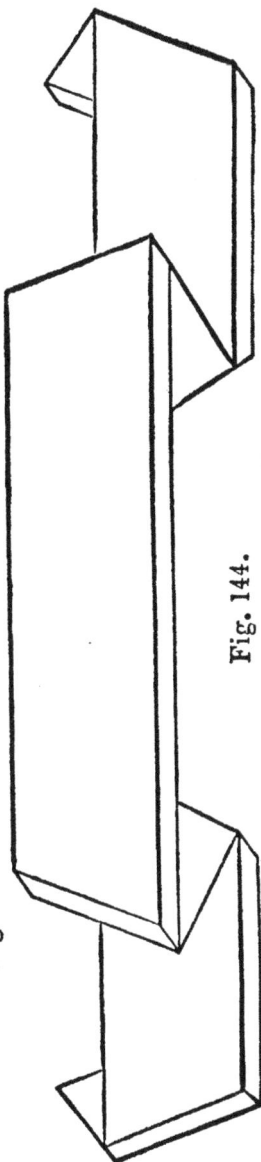

Fig. 141.

Fig. 142.

Fig. 143.

Fig. 144.

Figs. 141 to 144.—Scrolls.

It is desirable for the student to practise on the blackboard the series of outline subjects given with this
chapter until he is able to turn out a passable specimen
of each one. Fig. 139 is a plain board with a screw head
at each corner ; Fig. 140 a plain shield ; and Figs. 141,

Fig. 145.—Hand pointing horizontally.

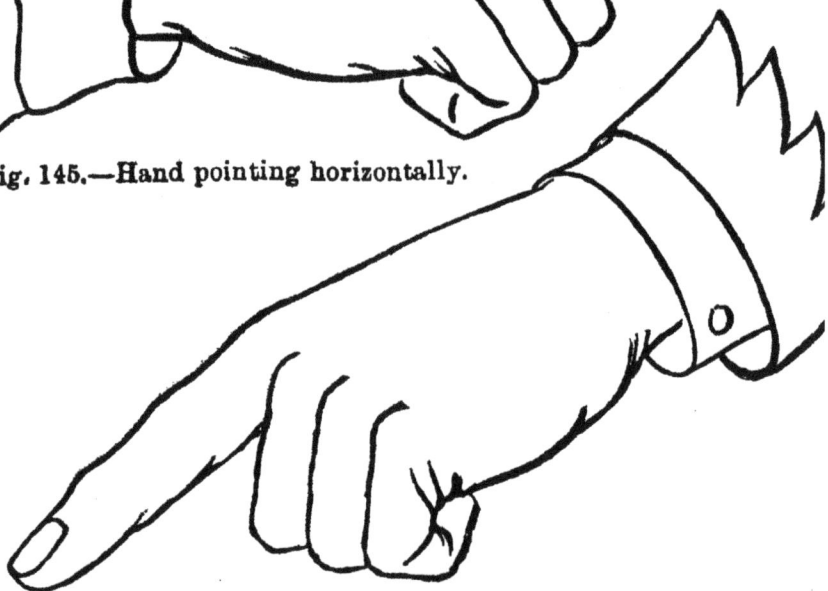

Fig. 146.—Hand pointing downwards.

142, 143, 144, a series of four scrolls. Figs. 145 and 146
are a pair of hands, one pointing in a horizontal direction and the other downwards.

   The Royal Arms (Fig. 147) will prove the most difficult subject of all, but as the sign-writer is frequently
called upon to paint it he must take it very seriously in
hand. After he has gained experience in the manipula-
tion of his brush, he will find it not so difficult as it at
first appears, and he will soon be able to draw it in

Fig. 147.—The Royal Arms.

Fig. 148.—Prince of Wales's Plume.

Fig. 149.—Centre Ribbon Ornament.

Fig. 150.—Crown.

Fig. 151.

Fig. 152

Figs. 151 and 152.—Scroll-work Corner Pieces.

proper proportions with great facility. The subject should be first drawn on the board with chalk in a somewhat sketchy manner, allowing freedom to the hand, and relying on the brush for putting in the lines in a firm, masterly way afterwards.

It need hardly be said the. Royal Arms is always

Fig. 153.—Branch of Lemon Tree.

Fig. 154.—Lemon Tree Conventionalised.

executed in gold and certain regulation heraldic colours. In painting this, or any other heraldic emblem, every part of the work is outlined with black, and shaded more or less. The gold is best shaded with burnt sienna, with a little burnt umber added ; and the white parts with Vandyke brown and ultramarine blue, or with blue-black alone ; the reds and blues with purple-lake, or burnt umber and crimson-lake. The colours of

coats of arms and all heraldic devices are fixed absolutely, and from these there can be no departure. The
Prince of Wales' Feathers (Fig. 148) is a much easier
subject. Perhaps it would be better to attempt this
first.

The Crown (Fig. 150) is more difficult, and a little
practice will be necessary to draw it to the correct shape.
Fig. 149 is a centre ribbon ornament, and Figs. 151 and
152 two scroll-work corner pieces.

Hotel signboards hardly come within the range of
the sign-writer, they belong to the sign-painting branch
of the craft. They are numerous and varied in style
and design. However, an example is given here, with a
brief description.

The Lemon Tree.—There is no appreciable difference
in foliage between this and the orange tree, but the
lemon is less bushy in growth ; the fruit is different in
form and colour. The annexed sketches will be sufficiently accurate for general purposes. Fig. 153 shows
the actual growth, Fig. 154 is the tree conventionalised
to fill the required space. The fruit should be made
rather extra big, and the trunk, fruit, and leaf should
have a bold black outline. The fruit, to make an effective sign, should be gilded, and it may be shaded up
with wash-black mixed with a dash of verdigris and
Prussian blue. The leaves should be of a dark green,
something the colour of the laurel. The Moorish arch,
as sketched, will be filled by the tree—better than a
Roman arch. It will also be more appropriate, as being
that of the countries where lemon trees grow.

CHAPTER VIII.

TICKET-WRITING.

By attention to the following directions, anyone pos-sessed of the requisite patience will be enabled to master the general principles which underlie the craft of ticket-writing, and, by subsequent steady practice, will acquire proficiency in all its details.

For a successful commencement the following tools and materials will be wanted :—

Brushes.—The best are made of sable-hair. If small writing is to be done, the size known as " crow " (Fig. 44, p. 36), costing 4d. each, will be best. When learning, however, it will be necessary to write the letters large ; just as in penmanship a good style can only be acquired by practising large hand. If only one brush is to be bought, a " goose " (Fig. 47, p. 36) will perhaps be the best size to select ; this will cost 1s. 3d. in sable. For larger work, it will be well to have " small swan " (Fig. 50), which, in sable, costs 4s. 6d., but a camel-hair brush, costing 1s. 3d., will suit most purposes. The bodying-in of big letters can be done more quickly with a big brush. The ticket-writer's outfit of brushes might be considered complete for all kinds of writing if a " crow," a " goose," and a " small swan " are obtained. Very good work can be done with camel-hair or Siberian-hair brushes ; they are cheaper, but they do not work quite so easily as sable-hair ones.

In using the brush, it is particularly necessary, in order to produce clean, well-written work, to acquire facility in making slow, steady sweeps, and not, as is mostly the practice with beginners, to make a number of short, jerky, scratchy movements. This sweeping movement gives an even edge to the outlines of a letter, whilst short dabs only result in a saw-like jaggedness.

The whole secret of using the brush may be said to lie in acquiring this sweeping movement. The rule should be :—Never allow your brush to be or the outer edge of a letter unless it is travelling at a slow, even rate, in the direction of the outline at that part. Of course, a brush must of necessity be removed and replaced ; but before removing it, draw it away towards the centre of the letter ; when replacing it, let first contact take place at some central part, and from there commence the sweeping motion, so that when the outer edge is reached the hairs have settled themselves into shape for continuing an even-edged mark.

No amount of practice with the jerky method will make good ticket-writing, but with continuous sweeps, quickness as well as correctness are certain. Enough ink must be taken up to keep a decided pool always under the brush, so that when a fresh dip is made into the ink-pot the brush is not returned to a partially dry line. A spot once allowed to dry must not be gone over again until the whole letter of which it forms part has dried. A second coat will be found to be quite unnecessary in all but exceptional cases, where bad ink or a bad surface is in question.

If an outline of the writing is to be made first, this must be done in one of two ways. Either mark it lightly with a fine lead-pencil, or rule it with a drawing-pen and pen-compass. A broadish line should be used—perhaps $\frac{1}{32}$ in. wide. The curved portions must be put in first, and their extremities joined where necessary by straight ruling. When this ink is dry, begin to fill in with the brush. Whilst using the brush, do not keep turning the ticket round and round to bring successive sides of the letters parallel with a line joining your eyes ; draw the brush from above downwards, when filling in upright or approximately upright limbs, and from left to right when filling in horizontal or approximately horizontal limbs. Tickets, as a whole, should be begun in left top corner, and finished at bottom right corner.

Cardboard.—This is made in all thicknesses, and is called "two-sheet," "three-sheet," etc., according to the number of sheets that are pasted together to make it up. As a rule, the larger a ticket is to be the thicker should be the card on which it is written. The sheets in which card is sold also vary in size from "royal," 20 in. by 25 in., to "antiquarian," 30½ in. by 54 in., with intermediate sizes. Royal is the size mostly used, but any of the other sizes will do just as well. Card can be got in small or large quantities from any good stationery warehouse. A sheet can be cut into tickets, having lengths and breadths of widely varying proportions. For instance, a royal sheet will cut up into four long tickets 25 in. by 5 in., or into twenty square tickets 5 in. by 5 in., and, within the limits of the size of the sheet, into an endless variety of rectangular pieces. Much cardboard will be wasted unless heed is taken to cut economically : cutting pieces of useless widths or shapes is quite unnecessary in practice, and should be avoided.

Ink-pots or Dippers.—A separate ink-pot will be required for each colour and each kind of ink that is used. Any short, wide-mouthed bottle will do, having a stopper or cover that can be kept on to exclude dust and prevent evaporation when not in actual use. An ink-pot need not hold more than about an eighth of a pint.

A Board.—This need be only a piece of well-seasoned deal, without knots or cracks, 1 in. or more thick, and measuring 12 in. by 18 in. Both sides must be planed smooth and the edges squared.

Drawing-pins are not necessary. Get into the habit of using the cork support under your right hand when writing, and steady the card with two digits of your left.

A Hand-rest.—This consists of a piece of cork 4 in. by 3 in. by ¼ in., which can be got with the surfaces smooth as the cork-cutter's knife leaves them. A piece of tough brown paper must be glued to the top and another to the bottom of this cork and left to dry under pressure. When dry, the paper must be trimmed to the edges with a pair of scissors. Mark one side with some device, and always work with that uppermost. This rest is used under the hand, and keeps the ticket from getting moistened or dirtied by perspiration. It is light, and, at the same time, sufficiently thick to be easily picked up.

Card Cutters.—For these will be wanted a good pair of scissors with 4 in. blades ; a piece of stout plate-glass rather larger than the largest tickets intended to be written—the edges and corners of this had best be ground off ; a shoemaker's knife (Fig. 155), which must be kept sharp at the point by rubbing it upon a strip of

Fig. 155.—Shoemaker's Knife.

emery-cloth glued to a strip of wood, say 12 in. by 3 in. by 1 in., used as a barber uses a strop, but without any lubricant.

The sheet of glass mentioned above is used, in conjunction with the shoemaker's knife and metal straight-edge, to cut up card. The card is first ruled with pencil-marks to the sizes and shapes wanted. It is then laid, face up, on the glass, and the metal straight-edge is placed to coincide with the pencil-lines, and held firmly with the left, whilst the right hand draws the knife along the straight-edge. The knife's edge should be held at about 45°, and must sever the card at one cut ; a sharp point is, therefore, necessary.

Rulers.—A metal straight-edge ; two set-squares, one 45° and one 60° ; three wooden straight-edges, one 18 in., one 9 in., and one 6 in. long.

Measurers.—A pair of compasses, with pencil and pen ; a foot-rule divided into inches and fractions of an inch.

Markers.—A few soft lead-pencils, some sharpened to pin-points (as shown by Fig. 156), and some to chisel-shaped ends (as shown by Fig. 157), the points for outlining and marking freehand, the chisels for ruling lines; a pricker made by inserting a needle in a wooden handle with $\frac{1}{2}$ in. of the point projecting; a pounce, made by rolling a strip of flannel, 12 in. long and 3 in. wide, tightly into a roll and stitching it so; a drawing-pen; a sheet or so of tracing-paper.

The needle-point tool is for use with the pounce and tracing-paper. When a large number of similar tickets are wanted, or when it is desired to copy a letter quickly, a piece of tracing-paper is placed over it, and an

Figs. 156 and 157.—Lead Pencils.

outline made in pencil. This is then removed, placed over a thick cloth laid on a table and pricked through with holes, making a perforation like that used in sheets of postage-stamps. A perforating wheel (Fig. 158) will do this expeditiously. Some charcoal is reduced to a fine powder and placed in a saucer. The pounce is held upright, and its end dabbed into the charcoal powder. The perforated tracing-paper is placed over a card so that the perforations come where the outline of the writing is to appear. The pounce is then dabbed along the perforation, and by this means the charcoal dust is sent through, and black marks appear on the card beneath. A puff of breath will remove surplus charcoal dust from the ticket, and the writing can then be proceeded with direct, or the dotted line pencilled over first, if thought necessary.

Miscellaneous.—A slate and slate-pencil; a piece of soft indiarubber. The slate and pencil are used to make trial letters and tickets on, and will save the waste of much paper. In learning ticket-writing, it is not easy to know exactly where to commence the lines, how many words to place in each line, how wide apart the several lines should be, and what sized letters to use for each word, in order to make the most effective ticket. By experiment upon a slate, all this can be ascertained, and a more or less finished outline of the ticket made. Tracing-paper and pounce will then allow of it being transferred to the card, and the remainder is then easy enough. Gradually the slate will be found becoming unnecessary: this will be when tickets can be outlined upon it without requiring alteration; then, of course, the outlining can be done in lead-pencil

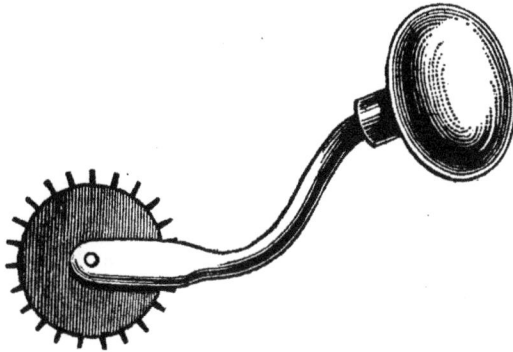

Fig. 158.—Perforating Wheel.

directly upon the card, and the slate can be put aside. Later on, when greater proficiency is attained, the pencil can in the same way be dispensed with, and the ink-brush used at once upon the clean card. In copying the ticket upon tracing-paper from the slate, only the outlines of the letters and figures must be drawn; guide-lines, although absolutely necessary at first to the beginner when working on the slate, are not wanted on the ticket itself. Great care must be taken to trace and prick the outline correctly.

To begin writing, take the slate, and draw upon it two parallel lines, say $2\frac{1}{4}$ in. apart; never work with small letters at first. Suppose we decide to write WORK between these guides:—first add up the number of letter widths (*See* Chap. II.) that are required for the word. To begin this, it must be first decided what width the ordinary letters are to be. Suppose this is decided upon as 1½ in. The height is now nine quarters, and the width six quarters of an inch. Consider, then, the quarter-inch to be our unit for measurements. Suppose we decide to have the limb-width one-sixth of the height, it will be 1½ units or ⅜ in. We will arrange to have our word in the middle of the slate. The letter-widths will be 1½ in. for O, R, and K, but W requires four-thirds of 1½ in., or 2 in. There must be a space between each letter ; this is equal between the extreme limits of every letter, whether I or W. To get a fair readable-looking word, we will have a space of ½ in. between the letters. The total letter-widths and spaces together come to $2'' + 1\frac{1}{2}'' + 1\frac{1}{2}'' + 1\frac{1}{2}'' + \frac{1}{2}'' + \frac{1}{2}'' + \frac{1}{2}'' = 8''$.

Find the middle point of the slate between the parallels already ruled. On each side of this point, 4 in. from it, draw a line at right angles to the parallels, to close their ends. Now, at intervals of ¼ in. between the parallels and at right angles to them, draw a number of lines. The first eight of these will be taken up by W, then two will go for a space, then six for O, two for a space, six for R, two for a space, and six for K. Now draw the letters in outline according to the rules given in Chap. II. When completed, carefully trace the word on tracing-paper, and, by using pricking-needle and pounce, transfer it to a clean card. This outline can then be filled in with brush and ink. From this word it is but a step to the writing of a complete ticket.

Never crowd letters, words, or lines together, nor put the writing as a whole upon a card that is too small for its proper display, and be careful to give a proportionate margin. Where possible, the rule should be followed to allow a space of from one-third to one-half a common letter-width between each letter, and twice as much between each word. Between lines allow a space at least equal to a quarter of the height of the tallest of the letters in the two lines it separates. More or less than these proportions often cannot be helped, but by observing them, a clear, easily-read ticket can always be depended upon. Around the writing allow a margin of clean card twice as wide as the widest space between any two lines inside.

Never copy inferior examples: large print, in good ink, on good paper, is the best thing to be got, although the spacing is often rather faulty. Collections of alphabets are sold by several publishers, and a selected set of these will afford a host of good examples. At any rate, obtain first-rate specimen letters only, and copy, copy, copy.

When writing tickets, conform to the orthodox spelling; always keep a reliable dictionary by you for reference when in doubt. However well a ticket may be written, a word spelled wrongly will make it ridiculous.

Do not work in semi-darkness if it can possibly be avoided. The defects that will be likely to creep in if you do will be shown up to their fullest extent when they come to be placed in the strong light of a shop window.

For all business purposes it will be found sufficient to use black, red, and blue, with white for writing on black and dark-coloured card. Any other colours may be added at discretion, it being only necessary to buy the right pigments; and the colourman will tell a purchaser what is most suitable.

Tickets intended for exposure to the weather are best varnished all over. The written ticket is given a couple of coats of isinglass solution, made by dissolving 1 oz. in 1 pint of boiling water; then mastic varnish or copal varnish is applied. A large flat brush is best for coating tickets, as it must be done rapidly. Varnished tickets look better and last longer than those which only have the writing done in waterproof ink.

Metal Tickets, such as are used by butchers, green-grocers, fishmongers, etc., are written upon tin-plate with oil-paint, and afterwards they are often varnished.

When written, a ticket should be allowed to dry slowly, and should be placed aside out of the way of dust and dirt. Warming and other hastening processes result in wrinkling, scorching, and smudging. When, beyond question, the ink is dry, any pencil-marks must be removed by light touches with soft indiarubber.

Ink is best and cheapest when bought ready-made, but as many readers of this Handbook may like to make ink for their own use, the following recipes and formulas are given.

Gum Arabic in solution forms the best vehicle for all indoor ticket-writing—that is to say, when the ticket is not to be exposed to rain, as is often the case with writing affixed to the outsides of shopkeepers' plate-glass windows. The liquid gum only needs the addition of a pigment to form ink : to this a drop or two of oxgall is added in the case of colours to brighten them up ; not too much, or the reverse effect will be brought about. The gum arabic solution is made by selecting only such pieces of gum as are quite clear, clean, and transparent. These are dissolved by pouring upon them cold water in the proportions of a quarter of a pint to one ounce. Should the liquid not be clear and colourless, it can be rendered so by placing in it about an equal quantity of freshly-made animal charcoal, coarsely powdered, and shaking up the solution for two or three minutes. The charcoal is removed by filtering through blotting-paper, the liquid that passes being colourless. It is essential that the charcoal should be freshly-made animal charcoal. To obtain this, get some bones—say a sheep's rib-bones—and saw them into pieces about an inch long. Bury these in a flower-pot, plugged at the bottom with clay and filled with silver-sand, and place in a fire or Bunsen flame. By uncovering now and then, the carbonising process can be watched, and when complete, the sand can be emptied out, the bones gathered together, and coarsely powdered with a pestle in a mortar. Blow away the fine dust, or it will clog the filtering paper.

Colours.—The following pigments are used to colour the gum solution :— *Vermilion* is the best red for general purposes, it costs 4d. an ounce when of good quality—a larger quantity of gum is wanted with it. *Cobalt* is the best decided blue ; it costs 1d. an ounce. *Emerald Green* is unsatisfactory to mix at home, and should be bought in the tube and gum solution added to thin it. Indeed, when only a little ticket-writing is going to be done, it is cheapest, cleanest, and least trouble to buy tubes of colour and then thin it with gum solution. For *Black* get a halfpennyworth of vegetable black. For *Gold* ink buy gold leaf, sold in books each containing twenty-five leaves, 3¼ inches square, interleaved with tissue. Grind a leaf up with gum solution on the slab, adding water to thin it. Dutch metal, something like gold, but tarnishing quickly, costs only 1d. a book. Bronze powders of various shades, gold, green, purple, red, yellow, etc., can be got at an oilshop and of artists' colourmen. Very little gum solution should be used in mixing bronze powders. They are better dusted on a coat of nearly dry (sticky) gum solution, or, better, on a coat of gold size ; the metallic dust is very hurtful to one's lungs if inhaled.

All the above colours are bought dry, ready ground to powder. A sufficient quantity is tipped out on a slate or glass slab, and ground with a palette-knife. Enough gum solution is then added to make a treacly liquid. This is placed in an ink-pot, and diluted with more gum solution, adding a drop or two of prepared ox-gall and enough water to make a thin ink that will work well with the brush. A few drops of oil of cloves will prevent the moulding of the ink and give it a pleasant scent. Quite a passable black ink can be made by detaching a little soot from a blackened paraffin-lamp chimney, and mixing it with some liquid gum on a sheet of glass, using a palette-knife to incorporate the two, and, if necessary, adding water to thin it.

To make glossy ticket ink use very little colour to the liquid gum arabic. Try for quality by putting a dab on a waste piece of card, and seeing how it dries.

Waterproof Black Ink is made as follows :—To half a pint of boiling water add half an ounce of powdered borax and one ounce of shellac. Place this over the fire, and keep stirring till shellac and borax are all dissolved Stir in just so much vegetable black as is necessary to colour the solution a deep black, without making it thick. Strain, when quite cold, through an old handkerchief. More shellac will make it glossier, more borax will make it less liable to chip off the card when written. A little indigo added will make the black less of a brown.

Waterproof Coloured Inks. — (1) For small, stiff tickets, write with the ordinary ink, and varnish with spirit varnish applied with a large, soft, flat brush very carefully. When the varnish dries, the surface will be impermeable to wet. Give more than one coat of varnish if necessary.

(2) Gelatine melted in hot water, and then having enough vermilion added to produce the required shade of red. When wanted, the gelatine ink should be stood in hot water and melted, stirring up the colour if sunk to the bottom.

(3) Either gelatine or size mixed with vermilion and melted in hot water. Bichromate of potash, dissolved in as little hot water as is necessary, is added to small quantities of this ink a few minutes before it is used. The ink must then [be used at once in a room dimly lighted. When tickets written with this ink are exposed to strong sunlight for an hour or more, the ink becomes non-absorptive of water, and remains fast against rain, etc. The objection to this ink is that, whether it dries in the pot or on a ticket, it cannot be dissolved again by water after light has fixed it.

(4) For small tickets, bleached shellac dissolved in spirit of wine and coloured with any of Judson's dyes will make a moisture-proof writing material. This is expensive when large quantities are used. It evaporates from the bottle, too, rather quickly.

(5) Get some white hard spirit varnish from an

oilshop, and store it in a very soundly corked bottle. Dissolve in a little spirit of wine any of Judson's aniline colours (blue, red, yellow, etc., sold in penny packets also at oilshops). Add the coloured spirit to the required quantity of varnish, and use quickly, preferably in a cold room, as a warm atmosphere so soon dries the writing.

The following method may be employed to make waterproof ink of any colour, where the pigments will not be spoilt by its use :—Grind the colours up with a little gelatine dissolved in hot water, and then add a little bichromate of potash. The ink must be kept from evaporating, as it cannot be again dissolved after having once dried and been exposed to daylight.

An ink for writing upon linen, holland, calico, etc., is made as follows :—Vegetable black 1, gold size 2, turpentine 3, and boiled oil rather less than 1 part. When a colour is used, the proportions are : boiled oil 2, gold size 2, turpentine 5, to one of colour.

To prepare Oxgall for Ticket-writing.—(1) Evaporate fresh oxgall to a syrup, and then pour it in to a shallow tray, and set it by the fire to dry. Prepared in this way, the stuff will keep indefinitely in stoppered bottles. (2) It can be evaporated to dryness in a water bath. Treatment with alcohol will precipitate the mucus and epithelium. (3) Boil one pint of fresh oxgall with 1 oz. of alum. In another vessel, another pint with 1 oz. of table salt. After these have stood for three months the clear portion from each is mixed for use. The colour can be removed from oxgall by slightly acidulating it with one or two drops of acetic acid, and then passing through it a stream of chlorine gas or nascent oxygen. Considering the very small quantity used in ticket-writing on a small scale, it hardly pays to make it.

CHAPTER IX.

POSTER PAINTING.

THE materials required for poster painting will be com-
prised in paper, colours, brushes, and a few other tools,
such as compasses, tracing wheel, straight-edge, gauges,
etc. The brushes should be of the best quality At
least six will be needed for quickness when working
with several colours. Having a brush in each colour
saves a lot of trouble and saves the delay caused by
stopping to wash out brushes. Poster painting must be
done quickly in order to be remunerative. One lining
brush, or preferably two, of different sizes will be required ; these are bevelled brushes of the shape shown
in Fig. 159 : At the least four flat fitches, as shown at
Fig. 160, are also wanted. These should range in size from
about $\frac{3}{4}$ in. to $1\frac{1}{4}$ in. wide—these would be known as
Nos. 9, 10, 11, 12.

The tracing wheel is a brass wheel with steel points,
$\frac{3}{16}$ in. or less apart, sticking out around it (Fig. 158).
In use the ball handle is held firmly in the hollow of
the hand, the wheel is run round the designed letter and
the points will pierce as many as eight sheets of paper,
thus outlining eight letters at once.

Compasses are generally large : the way to make
them is as follows :—

Take two pieces of clean wood, free from knots, cut
a mortice in one and a tenon in the other, as shown in
Fig. 161 ; cut the square parts as shown in Fig. 162. A
screw is then inserted at A, Fig. 161, and the two pieces
put together, forming the tool shown in Fig. 163. The
use of the compasses will be obvious at once.

Straight-edges made of strips of wood $\frac{3}{4}$ in. thick, $2\frac{1}{2}$ in. wide, and up to 5 ft. long are used.

Gauges are flat strips of wood about 18 in. long and of a width corresponding with that of the ordinary letters you may have to form. The gauge is laid upon the paper, and by making a pencil mark on both sides the width of letter is at once traced. This facilitates the work. An ordinary carpenter's pencil is good for this

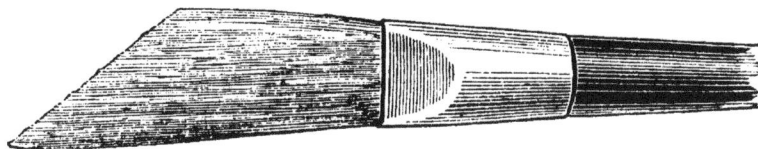

Fig. 159.—Lining Brush.

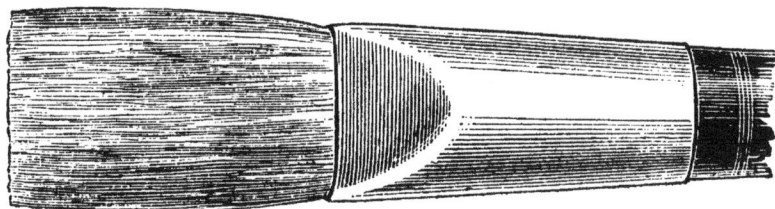

Fig. 160.—Flat Fitch.

purpose—it makes a bold line, and is not liable to break.

The paint used for posters is usually printers' ink thinned with benzoline, adding a little terebine, which hardens the colour as it dries. Some colours dry much slower than others. Black is especially a slow drier, and wants a little gold-size to hasten it. Blue is not a quick drier. All reds and yellows are, as a rule, good driers. In thinning out the ink, a little judgment in working will show when the right consistency is attained. To make colour dry with a gloss on it, use varnish in the mixing. If paper varnish is used instead of benzoline, turpentine must be used for thinning. Add this little by little, trying the colour after each addition; too much turpentine is liable to spread from the colour, staining the paper round the letters.

With any other varnish, benzoline will do for thinning,
but benzoline mixed with paper varnish, turns solid and
cannot be used. If printers' ink cannot be obtained,
grind up dry colours with varnish, and thin out the same
with either benzoline or turpentine.

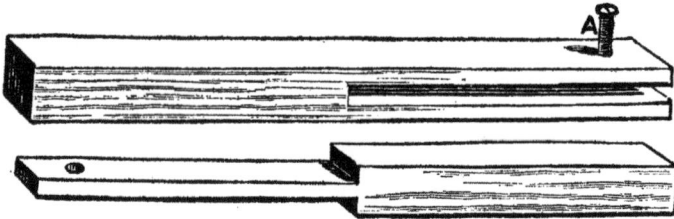

Fig. 161.

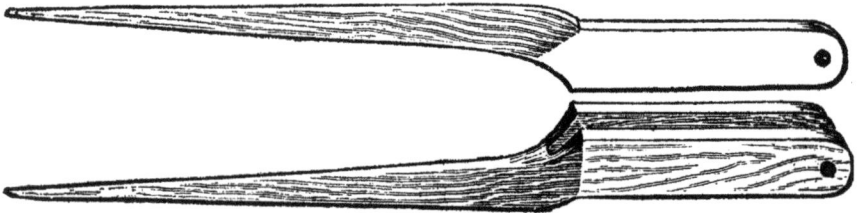

Fig. 162.

Fig. 163.

Poster Painters' Compasses.

The regular sizes of papers generally used for posters
are double-demy, 22½ in. by 34½ in., and double crown,
20 in. by 30 in. Smaller sizes are made by folding these
sheets. For poster painting it is best to have paper
that is not very thin, or the colour would sink in and
spoil before it dries.

Before we commence work, everything must be
systematically arranged because so much depends on
quickness. In the room to be used for the purpose,
have lines stretched from wall to wall to hang the
posters on, so that they may dry as they are painted. In
the middle of the room, have a table with a board the

size of the sheets being worked on, raised about 4 in. at the back to give it the slope of a desk. On one side have pots of colour arranged handy, with a spatula—that is, a piece of flat wood (see Fig. 164)—in each pot, to keep the colours well mixed, and a brush in each colour in use. Paper, straight-edge, compasses, wheel, etc. should also be arranged handy and ready for use.

To paint double-crown size letters—that is, each letter to fill one sheet of double-crown—select the first letter of the first word and count the total number of such letters that are wanted, and count out a sufficient number of sheets of paper. Take not more than the tracing wheel will prick through, and lay them on the board.

Fig. 164.—Spatula.

With a pencil draw the letter on the top sheet, then with the tracing wheel run over all the lines, pressing it firmly so as to prick through the whole of the sheets. Draw the outline of the letters with the guidance of a straight-edge and lining brush, then fill in with broad fitches. A boy can do the filling in, and thus a great quantity of work may be got through in a day. As each letter is finished, hang it on a line. By the time all the lines are full, the sheet first put on should be thoroughly dry.

Red letters filled in around with black as a back-ground show up well. Rustic letters look well. Brown and green high lights touched up with lemon chrome is another effective letter ; and striped letters representing Scotch plaids are good. Shaded letters, the different colours being softened one into the other, are also showy —in fact, so much variety can be done in this line that it is only limited by the taste and judgment of the artist.

Single letters on single sheets of paper are easier to manage than having to put two or more letters on each sheet.

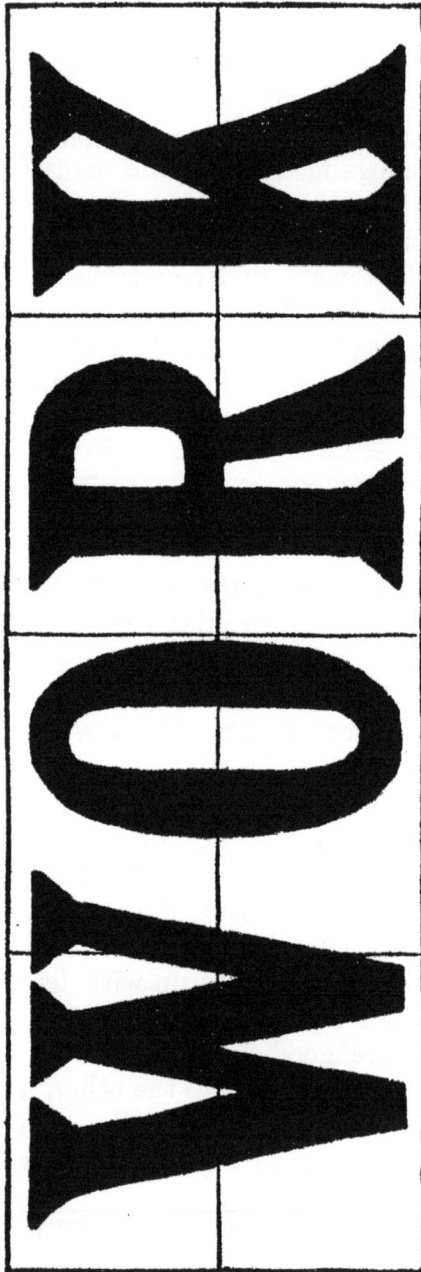

Fig. 165.—Eight-sheet Double-crown Poster.

Supposing you have a large poster to do—plan it out to scale on one sheet of paper, squaring out the number of sheets your poster is to contain (see Fig. 165). Now ascertain how many lines the matter to be dealt with

Fig. 166.—Single Letter on Two Sheets of Double-crown.

will take. See how many letters there are in the words to be displayed on each line, and divide the line into parts according to the size of the letters. Draw each letter, leaving a set space between each and an extra space between each word.

Fig. 165 shows the word WORK, divided to fill a poster consisting of eight sheets of double-crown. Fig. 166 shows, on an enlarged scale, two sheets of the same poster upon which the letter R appears.

According to the letters and their exact positions on the squares of the small design, so will they appear on the large sheets (see Figs. 165 and 166), the small squares represent the large sheets that are to be used. Fig. 166 shows two double-crown sheets held together with two tacks or drawing pins while the first copy is being drawn in, afterwards as many as are wanted are marked with the tracing wheel.

For small posters, say 6 ft. or 8 ft. square, stick together sheets of paper by pasting the edges, overlapping each other about ½ in. A good material to procure is lining paper; it may be bought at any shop dealing in wall papers; a roll of 12 yds. costs 7d. or 8d. This cut into lengths is much easier to handle than having smaller sheets to work with.

After a little practical knowledge is gained, poster painting is work that will be found easy, pleasant, and remunerative; and it affords plenty of scope in forming new designs and letters.

CHAPTER X.

LETTERING WITH GOLD.

THE tools and materials used by the sign-writer in gilding letters here mentioned are those generally used in letter-work.

The materials used for gilding, real or imitation, are— (1) genuine gold leaf ; (2) alloyed gold ; (3) Dutch metal ; and (4) bronze powders.

Genuine gold leaf always contains a certain amount of alloy, as pure gold is too ductile to be worked between the gold-beater's skin. It is sold in books of twenty-five leaves at about 1s. 4d. each, and gilders' work is measured and estimated by the hundred leaves. There are three shades of gold leaf sold—(a) very pale, (b) medium or yellow, (c) deep gold ; (b) is most suited for the sign-writer ; it looks best when varnished, and is the most durable if left unvarnished. It also stands the best against atmospheric influences when used on outside work. Gold leaf must be kept in a dry place ; if allowed to get damp, it will be impossible to re-move it from the book without tearing. Damp also tarnishes the leaf, and if any is found to be in this condition it should not be used, as it will spoil the work. Gold leaf should fall freely from the book on to the cushion by a gentle breath from the operator ; if it does not do so it is damp, and should be placed in front of a fire for an hour or so to dry it.

Letters for gilding upon are written in oil gold size, procurable at any colour shop. There is a slow and a quick drying size ; the former is prepared by grinding up fat linseed oil and yellow ochre ; a quick-drying varnish, with a little oil gold size added to it to keep it tacky, is a good preparation for the latter. By regu- lating the quantity of oil put with the varnish, it may be made to dry in three or four hours. Japanners' gold size and picture-frame-gilders' size may also be used for lettering.

The gilders' cushion (Fig. 167) is most important as a suitable surface to manipulate the gold upon. It is a wooden slab about 8 in. by 5 in., padded and covered with a soft leather. A piece of parchment is tacked round one end, and half round the two sides, as shown in the illustration. This is to prevent the gold leaf from being lifted off the cushion, as a slight breath of

Fig. 167.—Gilders' Cushion.

air is sufficient to carry it away. The cushion is held in the left hand by a leather loop, through which the thumb is inserted. There is also a smaller loop for holding the palette-knife when not in use.

The knives (Fig. 168) consist of a long blade in a handle, and have a hard, smooth, but blunt edge. They must be kept clean and bright, otherwise they will tear the leaf instead of cutting it. They are used to cut the gold to the required size and shape.

The " tip " (Fig. 169) is a thin layer of camel's hair glued between two pieces of cardboard, and is used for lifting the gold leaf from the cushion, and carrying and attaching it to the spot to be gilded. It is 4 in. wide, and varies in length, the most useful being 1 in., 1½ in., and 2 in.

Fig. 168.—Gilders' Knives.

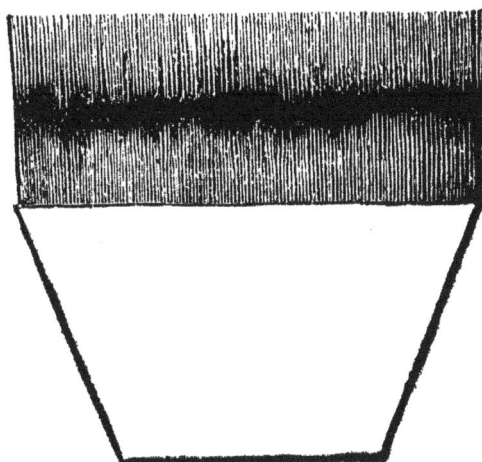

Fig. 169.—Gilders' Tip.

Fig. 170.—Gilders' Mop.

The gilders' mop (Fig. 170) is either flat or domed; it is used to dab the gold with, in order to make it adhere firmly to the prepared surface.

These are all the important tools that are really required, but a variety of sable, camel's hair, hog's hair pencils, and "skewing" may come into request in practice. Powdered chalk, tied up securely in a piece of fine muslin to make a pounce bag, for dusting on the painted surface is wanted. Sponges, dusters, and other requisites should also be kept specially for this work, and the whole of the tools and materials are best kept in a compact tin box.

The few necessaries required for letter gilding having been enumerated, the student may now be taken through the process of writing and gilding a sign in simple unshaded letters on a black ground. The first thing to do is to prepare the painted surface of the sign so that the leaf will be prevented from sticking anywhere except upon the desired portion—that is, the letters.

A sign which is to contain gilded letters, which are afterwards to be varnished, is always finished with a coat of "flatting," and on this surface there is not much chance of the gold adhering except upon the letters themselves. If the edges are not sharp and clear the sign must be "egg-sized" just round the letters. But many people will not have their gilded letters varnished over, as it takes so much off the brilliancy and richness of the gold. In such a case the sign has to be painted, varnished, and finished in every respect before the gold letters are put on. Varnish of the best and hardest drying quality procurable should be used, and allowed to set quite hard ; it can be left for a week after being applied to the sign-board. When hard, commence by removing every trace of dust by sponging the board over with cold water ; this will remove a certain amount of greasiness from the varnish ; when dry set out the letters in pencil, not in pipe-clay, and then dust round with the pounce bag containing powdered chalk. This need not be done lavishly, as is frequently the case, but the chalk should be carefully applied to the spaces between the letters, and for an inch or two above and below the letters. This chalk is, of course, to prevent the gold from sticking anywhere except to the letters, and to give these a sharp, clear edge. A very slight dusting should be sufficient, and it must not obliterate the outline of the letters. Should any chalk grit get upon the letters, it must be carefully dusted off with a small brush before applying the size, which is now got into a workable state.

Oil gold size sold in the little jars by oil and colourmen is generally too thick, and requires thinning to the proper consistency. This is done with boiled linseed oil, and strained through a fine piece of muslin into a small jar for use. Slow-drying size is laid on one day and gilt the next, but one of the quick-drying mordants is used if the gold leaf is to be laid on the same day as the size is applied.

Pouncing the sign with chalk, though a somewhat dirty and untidy method of working, is the one in general use ; some writers, however, use egg-size instead, which is prepared in this way :—The white of a fresh egg is mixed with a little water, and the whole whisked up into a froth with a clean new sash tool. This is applied over the entire surface of the sign, and will prevent stray particles of gold from sticking upon any part of the board. After the gilding is completed, the egg-size is washed off with a sponge and warm water.

Having thus prepared the sign-board and gold-size and marked out the letters, take a suitable sable pencil and fill them in with the size, and leave it to get nearly dry. The great point, which is somewhat difficult for the novice to determine, is when the size is ready to take the leaf. If the size is too moist and tacky, the gold will sink into it, and lose its brilliancy, besides showing every joint and looking dirty in places. If the size has got hard and lost most of its tackiness, the gold will not adhere properly. The state of the atmosphere affects the drying, and as the drying qualities of different sizes vary a sharp eye must always be kept upon the work. A very slight tackiness will cause the gold to adhere, and this is all that is required.

Supposing the size is now right, we proceed to apply

the leaf by the tip and cushion process. Take up the book of gold leaf, open the first leaf, and, breathing very gently at the edge of the leaf, hold the book at the same time close down to the cushion, so that the leaf shall fall upon it.

Take the cutting knife (Fig. 168), wipe it free from moisture, and cut the leaf into sizes suitable to the width of the letters. Dexterity is required in using the knife. Next take the tip (Fig. 169), lay it lengthways upon the leaf, and gently carry it from the cushion on to the sized letter; this operation is repeated until the whole letter is gilded, when it is very lightly dabbed over with a piece of cotton wool, the mop, or the dabber, according to fancy. The remaining letters are treated in this way and the job is finished. This method of gilding is certainly best, but it can seldom be employed in the open air. The gold leaf laid upon the size without pressure has much greater brilliancy than when laid on from tissue paper or from the book. When pressure must be used, it is liable to disturb the size and press the gold into it, and cause uneven work.

In outdoor gilding sign-writers of the old school take up a book, turn back the paper leaves, and without any cutting, place the leaf direct against the sized letter; this is a wasteful way of going to work, as with the slightest wind a great deal of the gold is wasted. The slightest movement in the air renders it very difficult to proceed so, when gilding out of doors, the sign-writer is generally shielded from the evil effects of the wind by a large coarse sheet.

The easiest of all methods in gilding is with the transfer gold leaf, as this leaf is easy to handle. Open the book at the first page and with the left hand take out the tissue square with the metal attached, place it with the gilded side on to the letter, and with the right hand gently rub it with a piece of cotton wool, on that portion which you wish to adhere; remove the tissue and apply the remaining leaf to another portion of the letter until all the gold is used up.

INDEX

Lightning Source UK Ltd.
Milton Keynes UK
UKHW010644131221
395574UK00001B/115

9 781528 702959